Johnnie Cochran

ATTORNEY

Black Americans of Achievement

LEGACY EDITION

Muhammad Ali

Maya Angelou

Josephine Baker

Johnnie Cochran

Frederick Douglass

W.E.B. Du Bois

Marcus Garvey

Savion Glover

Alex Haley

Jimi Hendrix

Langston Hughes

Jesse Jackson

Scott Joplin

Coretta Scott King

Martin Luther King, Jr.

Malcolm X

Bob Marley

Thurgood Marshall

Jesse Owens

Rosa Parks

Colin Powell

Chris Rock

Sojourner Truth

Harriet Tubman

Nat Turner

Booker T. Washington

Oprah Winfrey

Black Americans of Achievement

LEGACY EDITION

Johnnie Cochran

ATTORNEY

Gloria Blakely

CHELSEA HOUSE
PUBLISHERS
An imprint of Infobase Publishing

Johnnie Cochran

Chelsea House
An imprint of Infobase Publishing
132 West 31st Street
New York NY 10001

Library of Congress Cataloging-in-Publication Data

Blakely, Gloria.
   Johnnie Cochran : attorney and civil rights advocate / Gloria Blakely.—
Legacy ed.
     p. cm. — (Black Americans of achievement)
   Includes index.
   ISBN 0-7910-9112-0
   1. Cochran, Johnnie L. 1937-2005 2. African-American lawyers—United
States—Biography. I. Title. II. Series.
   KF373.C59B58 2005
   340.092—dc22   2005031752

Contents

The Trial of the Century

Attorney Johnnie Cochran was watching a slow-speed police chase on a news monitor in a local ABC studio. A caravan of Los Angeles police vehicles was following a white Ford Bronco on California Interstate 405. Inside the SUV was ex-football star O.J. Simpson, the LAPD's primary suspect in the July 12, 1994, murder of his ex-wife, Nicole Brown, and her friend Ronald Goldman. The slow-speed chase ended hours later when Simpson surrendered to the police at his Brentwood home. Relieved by the peaceful arrest, Cochran then appeared on Ted Koppel's *Nightline* television show. He cautioned viewers that, in accordance with American tradition, Simpson should be presumed innocent of the killings.

Much of the news had implied otherwise since the murders of Nicole Brown and Ronald Goldman. Juicy tidbits published about any suspect before he is arrested often come from one or more people involved in investigating the case. From

1

The white Ford Bronco carrying O.J. Simpson, above, is trailed by police cars as it travels on a California freeway on June 17, 1994.

the way the case was playing out, Cochran was worried that the leaks originated somewhere in the city's legal system and therefore indicated that Simpson had been the police's only suspect since day one.

ON THE SIDELINES

Like most Americans, Cochran first learned from television reports that Nicole Brown and an unidentified man had been slain. The attack occurred outside Brown's condominium in the Brentwood area of Los Angeles, while her two children slept upstairs undisturbed.

The *Today* show beamed this news into Cochran's bedroom, where he joined his wife, Dale Mason, early on the morning following the attack. He had finished his usual workout with his personal trainer in the gym in his home, a sanctuary that kept outside worries at bay. Cochran had been contemplating retiring from his busy law practice, or at least decreasing his workload. But that morning when Dale pointed out what was happening on the television, Cochran assumed he would get involved in the case. The story of the Brentwood murders related to someone he knew.

Though Cochran had never met Nicole Brown, her ex-husband was a casual acquaintance and fellow resident of Los Angeles. The two successful men and their families mingled in similar social circles. At events they both attended, Simpson was charismatic. He displayed outgoing, unpretentious warmth to which people always gravitated. Watching the reports of what had happened in Brentwood, Cochran immediately sympathized with Simpson's loss.

More news emerged about the slaying of Brown and the man identified as Ronald Goldman. Goldman waited tables at the Mezzaluna restaurant, where Brown had dined earlier that evening, and he was believed to be her friend. The public lapped up each detail. After all, this was the mysterious death of a beautiful, rich woman living in an upscale California neighborhood, a white woman linked to a black Hall of Fame football star and actor.

Cochran observed the situation with less than neutral feelings. It was rare for him not to be drawn into the legal activities of high-profile African Americans in Los Angeles. His legal wrangles on behalf of pop star Michael Jackson, football great Jim Brown, and TV star Todd Bridges proved how strong a reputation he held. Locals believed Cochran could win the unwinnable.

From day one, the media was in a frenzy. Cochran's phone rang continually. As a result, he appeared on *The Larry King Show* and *Nightline* to share his views.

O.J. Simpson phoned from jail soon after his arrest. He wanted Cochran on his defense team, but Cochran refused politely. He could not pledge the inordinate amount of time necessary for a criminal defense. He had enough work demanding his attention. If anything, he wanted to taper back his workload because he had already achieved what he had set out to do in his career. He had reached his business goals, and he had plenty of money to relax in the lifestyle of his dreams.

In addition, criminal cases were emotional wringers that placed a potentially innocent life in his hands. The building and managing of criminal cases haunted Cochran 24 hours a day. He spent his waking hours plotting strategy or preparing testimony; wishing for the best outcome interrupted his sleep. The Simpson trial, far from reducing his workload, would consume his mind and body for months.

Cochran signed a deal to be NBC's legal commentator for the duration of the case. The actions of Simpson's defense team, however, worried Cochran. Simpson's lawyers seemed like crisis managers during the preliminary hearing, rather than a team ready to mount an effective offense. They also let their client talk too much.

THEN CAME THE "DREAM TEAM"

Simpson's calls to Cochran were unrelenting. Cochran spoke with friends about taking on the case and finally decided to join in the defense. Simpson's team needed someone based in Los Angeles with trial experience, and Cochran was not the type of person to squander a major opportunity. The trial would be the biggest he had ever witnessed. At the very least, it promised to be an interesting challenge. Cochran wanted in the game.

Watching Simpson's original lawyers, led by Robert Shapiro, had been rough, despite the top-notch attorneys lending additional support. Noted trial attorney F. Lee Bailey advised the defense team from Florida, and Alan Dershowitz phoned in from Harvard Law School. Already Shapiro's group had no shortage of egos with opposing opinions.

Cochran's presence brought the team a new sense of purpose and cohesion. At first, he followed Shapiro's lead, but the more he came to know Shapiro, an entertainment attorney, the more his concern grew. Shapiro was known for dealing celebrities out of modest scrapes with the law, not trying major criminal cases. Shapiro's talk about earning $5 million from this case and his focus on press photos and celebrity gossip seemed far off base. Simpson, who was actively involved in all aspects of his defense, shared Cochran's concerns and also thought the case files appeared to be in disarray. He wanted Cochran to take charge but hesitated to upset Shapiro.

Other lawyers and members of the support team were disgruntled as well. F. Lee Bailey, Shapiro's friend, threatened to drop out before the trial. Simpson tended to avoid direct conflict but could skirt this issue no longer. Team meetings and case files had already been switched to Cochran's office. There, in the team's new location, leadership was formally transferred, despite Shapiro's protests. Cochran took charge of what became known as the "dream team."

The media attention to each step of the case offered the public unprecedented exposure to the American legal system. Not all of it was pretty. Cochran had learned as a Los Angeles county prosecutor that the system could be harsher and less just for a black man. This had prompted his decision to switch to the defense table decades before the Simpson trial; it was then that he launched his personal quest to reduce the effects of racism on the legal system. From the day his private practice opened, it never lacked defendants. The system kept generating hundreds of clients, with claims ranging from police brutality to racial profiling to the framing of innocent people. He recognized the Simpson case as another example of systemic bias—only this time, Cochran would be able to bring national attention to the issue.

Cochran started to chip away at the prosecution's evidence on January 31, 1995, after the first witness took the stand. Sharyn Gilbert, a 911 emergency dispatcher, spoke about Nicole Brown's pleas to save her from husband O.J.

Simpson six years earlier. The prosecution planned to emphasize evidence of alleged spousal abuse. Cochran had assigned himself this section of the defense. His goal was to either dispel insinuations about domestic violence or at least disassociate that alleged history from the Brentwood murders. Simpson may have had anger issues, but according to Cochran, he did not exhibit escalating violence, and he denied ever hitting Brown.

Rarely adversarial with opposing witnesses, Cochran kept his tone congenial and respectful with Gilbert. The prosecution attempted to disrupt his smooth flow with a torrent of objections. Nevertheless, Cochran exposed the fact that the dispatcher never spoke to anyone at the residence about physical abuse. She actually drew her conclusions regarding domestic violence not directly from Nicole Brown, but from hearing a male voice in the background of the telephone line. This was the prosecution's first hint of trouble. They were yet to realize how much would come, for there would be another party facing trial—the Los Angeles Police Department.

IN HIS OWN WORDS...

In the second of his two autobiographies, *A Lawyer's Life*, Johnnie Cochran opened the last chapter:

> My love for the promise of justice has never wavered, never, but a lifetime working the legal system has forced me to deal with reality. What we have in this country is the appearance of justice. Inside the courtroom everybody is dressed properly and stands respectfully in the correct place and uses the correct legal language and files the right papers, and it seems like justice for defendants. As a criminal defense lawyer I understood the system, I knew it well, and I used it for my client's benefit. That was my job and I did it.

RUSH TO JUDGMENT

Possibly no other witness devastated the prosecution's case as much as LAPD Detective Mark Fuhrman. Prosecutor Marcia Clark, a deputy district attorney, questioned Fuhrman when he took the stand. F. Lee Bailey cross-examined him for the defense. Months later, a series of tapes played in open court contradicted much of Fuhrman's testimony about his attitudes toward blacks and the lengths to which he would go to ensure a conviction. Jurors were left doubting Fuhrman's credibility and, more important, the validity of the evidence from his investigation. Racism, lying, and planting evidence became associated with the detective when the dream team was finished with him.

Well before Fuhrman raised his hand to swear to tell the truth, deputy district attorney Chris Darden was advised to stay away from the officer's testimony. "My brother," Cochran forewarned Darden, "I'm telling you don't get involved with Fuhrman's testimony. You have a life after this trial. You're black. Don't do it." After Fuhrman took the stand, even Darden and Clark tried to distance themselves from the detective's remarks. In closing statements, both attorneys cautioned the jury not to free Simpson because of "the racist attitudes of one officer."

IF IT DOESN'T FIT...

Cochran revisited those doubts during his closing arguments. Standing before a jury of diverse men and women, he raised gloved hands, reminding them of what happened in the first half of the trial. Deputy district attorney Chris Darden had asked Simpson to try on the gloves that supposedly linked Simpson to the murders. "Like the defining moment in this trial," Cochran said with confidence, "the day Mr. Darden asked Mr. Simpson to try on those gloves and the gloves didn't fit, remember these words: if it doesn't fit, you must acquit."

Johnnie Cochran, above, puts on a pair of gloves. This act was intended to remind the jury in the O.J. Simpson double-murder trial that the gloves Simpson tried on did not fit him.

Before Darden's display, Cochran and F. Lee Bailey had tried on the gloves and knew they would not fit Simpson. While the defense could have brought up the discrepancy in the gloves' sizes, Cochran thought the discovery would prove more dramatic for the jury if it happened when the prosecution was making its case.

Late in the prosecution's case, Cochran goaded Darden about the fit of the gloves and delivered other comments to shake the young prosecutor's composure. He kept up the pressure until cuing Bailey to offer a challenge Darden would not refuse. If the prosecution did not have Simpson try on the gloves, the defense would. Darden could not figure out what game they were playing. He took the bait.

In an interview, District Attorney Gil Garcetti said, "I was shocked—shocked—when I saw Chris Darden taking the glove out, because we had concluded no one's going to be trying that glove. It's too risky." Simpson donned the gloves as asked and the rest is history. The prosecution tried to recover by saying that Simpson had enlarged his hand muscles through exercise and that the gloves shrank during testing procedures, but none of these arguments could overcome what the jurors saw.

The pair of gloves was one of many elements troubling Cochran in what he characterized as a rush to prosecute Simpson for double homicide. "If it doesn't fit, you must acquit," best expressed the dream team's feeling about the prosecution's case. It naturally became the punctuating phrase in Cochran's closing arguments, for his use of the catchy rhyme was not accidental. Those words were calculated for maximum impact. "I often used rhymes in my summations," he wrote in his second autobiography, A Lawyer's Life. "I'd found that juries enjoyed them, understood them, and, most importantly, remembered them."

To simply say the jury remembered "if it doesn't fit" is an understatement. The line was parodied around the globe long after the murder case faded from TV screens. "I am unhappy to admit that few people have done as much for truly bad rhyming as I have," Cochran joked in A Lawyer's Life. That line and Cochran's name became household words. Together they helped pull off the coup that freed O.J. Simpson.

All that could outshine the infamous phrase and his celebrity client was Cochran's skills in the courtroom. Some people praised him for finally bringing justice to a black man. Others vilified him for letting an alleged killer run free. No one, though, could deny his legal brilliance in guiding the dream team to victory.

Cochran took pride in his work, and whether receiving compliments or being accused of playing the "race card," he wanted people to understand his motives. "We did not set out to put the police on trial," he wrote. "I am not anti-police—I am for police, for police doing their job properly, being honest."

In Simpson's case he truly believed that "the evidence that had been gathered by the police didn't fit the timeline the prosecution had established." To him, it did fit a pattern seen previously. "In the real world, as I've said, the police don't always tell the truth. They sometimes manufacture evidence. They sometimes plant evidence. They sometimes are biased. In that they are just like the rest of society."

What differed in Cochran is his belief that one man could transform a community. A single individual could open people's eyes and forge change. The perfect world may not result from his efforts. But if either one or a dozen lives were saved, it would be worth every ounce of sweat. It would be the job of a lifetime.

2

He's Always on Time

Johnnie L. Cochran, Jr., was born in Shreveport, Louisiana, the first child of Johnnie L. Cochran, Sr., and Hattie Cochran. Two daughters, Pearl and Martha Jean, would follow in the short space of three years.

The Cochran family was poor by American standards, but not so poor that the children would notice. They were in the same situation as others around them. Black Americans felt the economic pinch of the Great Depression first and were the last to see it pass. The Cochrans, though, took pride in keeping their children well fed. Hattie Cochran balanced hearty meals with a little dirt. Multi-vitamins were yet to arrive on the scene, so the occasional handful of soil rounded out their mineral intake. The family had money enough for a used car, which granted them the luxury of avoiding racially divided public transportation.

The photo above shows a view of Texas Street in Shreveport, Louisiana, the town where Johnnie L. Cochran, Jr., was born.

Playing with the daughter of his grandmother's white employer was one of the few exceptions in young Johnnie's decidedly black world. He and his sisters lived protected by the comfort of Baptist prayer, which encouraged them to believe in their own greatness.

DEEP ROOTS

When the sun rose, Johnnie awoke to the aromas of his mother's cooking. Hattie Cochran began each day in the kitchen. She enjoyed preparing traditional Southern meals for her family, which included Big Auntie, Johnnie's paternal grandmother, and Aunt Easter and her son, Arthur Lee, who lived with Johnnie and his family in a rented three-bedroom house. Johnnie learned the basics of arguing a case from family debates around the dinner table.

The extended family shared not only the white clapboard home, but also faith in a better future. This was the kind of future that inspired Johnnie's grandfather, Alonzo Crockrum, to see beyond his roots in slavery and, later, cash-poor sharecropping. To better suit the future he envisioned, Alonzo changed his birth name from Crockrum to the simpler Cochran. Alonzo and his wife, Hannah, named their son Johnnie Cochran. When he named his own son Johnnie, he added the middle initial "L.," which symbolized expectations that his son's education and job opportunities would surpass his own achievements.

Hannah and Alonzo Cochran worked six acres on a plantation owned by Will, Lee, Trigg, and Charles Hutchinson. White planters like the Hutchinsons had reconsolidated their economic and political strength following the Civil War. Ruling planters learned to minimize farm costs in ways not too distant from what occurred during slavery. Following Southern custom, the four Hutchinson brothers provided seed, farm equipment, and cabins to the Cochrans and other tenant farmers. When the cotton harvest was delivered, rent and equipment were first deducted from the tenant's share of the proceeds and the balance came in paper scrip redeemable at the general store, also owned by the Hutchinsons. Cash had to be earned through outside endeavors.

While the Cochrans did their best to earn a decent living, Johnnie lived with Alonzo's grandfather, David Brown, and went to school. Johnnie thrived at school, achieving the rank of valedictorian at age 14. He became the first of his immediate family to move to Shreveport, 20 miles north of their home, after outgrowing his rural education. He stayed with his upwardly mobile Aunt Lucille and her husband, Aristide Albert, while attending Central Colored High. There, he earned grades stellar enough for him to qualify to go to college. His outlook changed abruptly when his father died during harvest. Johnnie returned to the farm to finish the work on his father's crops.

HOLDING ON TO FAITH

With the harvest in and all debts settled, Johnnie, a child no longer, brought his mother to Shreveport. Together with her, cousin Arthur Lee, and his cousin's mother, Johnnie substituted family obligations for his dream of a college degree. Any further learning would have to be accomplished on his own. To help keep the household running, 18-year-old Johnnie found a job as a delivery boy for a Walgreen's drugstore. He and Arthur Lee pooled resources to buy a well-used car that often needed to be repaired. Still, the old clunker made his drugstore deliveries faster and enabled him to visit his high school sweetheart, Hattie Bass, frequently.

Hattie and Johnnie married in 1937. Johnnie Jr. was born on October 2, 1937. To better provide for his growing family and elevate his status in the community, Johnnie Sr. embarked on a career selling insurance for one of the largest black-owned businesses in the area, Louisiana Industrial Life Insurance Company. Getting the black community to place its trust and hard-earned money in a black establishment was a challenge that thrilled Johnnie Sr. Converting these skeptical buy-

IN HIS OWN WORDS...

In his autobiography *Journey to Justice*, Cochran wrote about one of the great lessons of human value taught by his father, Johnnie Cochran, Sr., the consummate insurance salesman:

He was a great salesman with an infectious spirit of optimism. Whenever I worked with him, I learned the importance of being an empathetic listener. I learned that people needed and wanted to hear good news, and that if you couldn't provide them with it, then the next best thing you could do for them was to let them know that better news was just around the corner. For my father, everything was doable and the word "impossible" did not exist. Life presented you with a series of challenges, and those who took advantage of opportunities, those who met the challenges head on, led the most fulfilling lives. Working with my dad, I learned to enjoy dealing with people. I began to thrive on "making a way out of no way."

ers was tantamount to sweeping aside the invisible remnants of slavery. His entrepreneurial work fit well with his and his wife's life philosophies: "Always be the best you can be," and "always recognize that all human endeavors are imperfect and incomplete. Perfection demands continuous study, growth, progress, and change." These words, instilled in the next generation of Cochrans, empowered Johnnie Jr. to become an A student.

Positive encouragement from his family, reinforced by the Baptist church, fueled not only the young boy's compassion and moral center, but also a thirst for continued success. Johnnie grew up believing he could be everything that he wanted to be if he planned well and worked hard. He counted on this attitude wherever life steered him. Because these philosophies also made his parents receptive to new and unexpected opportunities, one prospect would soon take them to San Francisco.

EMBRACING CHANGE

In 1942, the Cochran family moved to the San Francisco area. In December 1941, the United States became involved in World War II, and Johnnie Sr., who had become known as "Chief," wanted to contribute to the war effort in a manner that did not jeopardize his family's future. They could not afford to lose him in battle. When Aunt Lucinda came to visit from San Francisco, she brought along fascinating stories about palm-lined streets and booming industries short on employees. She said that the shipyards, in particular, offered equal job opportunities to blacks and whites. Equal jobs and equal pay were quite unusual at that time. The opportunity sounded too good to ignore.

Chief arrived in September. He found a job as a pipe fitter at Bethlehem Steel in the Alameda Naval Shipyards on the southeastern shore of San Francisco Bay and had a home waiting for his family in public housing nearby. Integration entered Johnnie Jr.'s life in Alameda's housing project and public education system, where African Americans, whites, and Latinos lived and attended school. This would be the first of many eye-opening changes for the boy.

Another change during the 1940s was blacks entering major league sports. Johnnie Jr. and his father took special pride in renowned black sports figures of the day. Without thinking about why it would occur, young Johnnie knew that when one black man made it into the big leagues, more were to follow. Jackie Robinson, although not the best player in Negro League baseball, was the first to integrate into the white Major League in 1947.

Johnnie's father said Robinson was chosen because he could "handle it." The young boy had no understanding of the "it" Robinson faced, for the Cochran household focused on unlimited horizons and building self-esteem, not the racism that fueled the curses that taunted Robinson and the threats on his life.

Cochran explained the family philosophy in his second book: "I don't remember ever feeling that my race was holding me back. . . . My father did not want any of his children using racism as an excuse for failure."

STRAIGHT AND NARROW

Johnnie was six years old when the family joined Beth Eden Baptist Church in Alameda. His father established himself there as a deacon, just as he had been in Shreveport. The Cochran household continued to uphold the discipline and respect originating in their Southern roots. Nothing less was tolerated from the children. The adage "be the best you can be" echoed through their California home, and Chief lived that statement, making time to study religion and write religious and philosophical poems each evening after work.

Young Johnnie followed his father's example and excelled at learning. He skipped second grade, but was reminded how much was expected of him when two or three B's appeared on

Jackie Robinson, above, was an infielder for the Brooklyn Dodgers and the first black man to play Major League baseball. He was one of Johnnie Cochran's sports heroes.

his elementary school report cards. His parents scrutinized each one and laid out a plan to turn them into A's. Nor were his two sisters excused from their parents' encouraging expectations. The children's futures received priority in the household, regardless of the ongoing demands of keeping a roof over their heads and food on the table.

Around this time, the physical and mental strength needed to raise a family began to register on young Johnnie. "Like any small child, I took my parent's strength for granted. In Alameda, I began to appreciate it and to develop a sense of just how valuable it was to all of us." He remembered seeing his father come home tired everyday from pulling double duty to support one of the largest naval fleets in World War II.

Chief would leave home in his steel-toed work boots after one of Hattie's Southern-style breakfasts and return home physically exhausted 12 hours later. No matter how tired he felt, he remained a role model as an attentive father and loving husband who used his spare time for self-education.

Johnnie's mother pulled double duty as well. She sold Avon cosmetics to neighbors whose wages from the shipyards permitted some discretionary spending. Two breadwinner households were commonplace among African Americans who, like the Cochrans, worked toward middle-class dreams.

THE NEXT MOVE UP

Middle-class dreams drew nearer when Johnnie's father received a job offer from the Golden State Mutual Insurance Company. World War II had come to an end, and as post-war defenses continued to wind down, shipyard layoffs were anticipated. Chief put away his tools before that could happen, and began to work for the largest black-owned insurance company in California.

This new job took the family south to San Diego in 1948. They said tearful farewells to everyone in Alameda. The children were upset by the move. They unpacked and found new spots for their belongings in a small, unfurnished two-bedroom apartment on Ocean View Boulevard. It appeared more like the Cochrans were starting from scratch than bettering themselves. The apartment's location failed to live up to the boulevard's scenic name. No ocean was in sight from their windows, but malodorous smells from canneries along the bay did blanket the area. At least for a short while, the Cochrans made the best of it.

Johnnie discovered some other differences in his new town. In San Diego he came across white soldiers and sailors who could not find a smile for a black boy. It was curious behavior, but the integrated school he attended compensated for their indifference. There were also occasional Sunday visits to cousins and uncles living in Watts, which was a proud black suburb of Los Angeles at that time. Equally, if not more satisfying, were Sunday services in San Diego at the local church, Bethel Baptist.

During one service when Johnnie was about 11 years old, the Reverend Charles Hampton recited John 3:16, a Bible passage the boy had heard before. This time, the words "for God so loved the world, that he gave his only begotten Son" had a different effect. Johnnie committed his life to Christ. From that day he promised to live according to the Lord's teachings and later wrote, "I've sometimes failed to live up to that agreement, but I've never regretted it."

Johnnie's awareness of the accomplishments of African Americans grew during this period. Blacks were appearing in films exploring interracial conflict, like *Lost Boundaries*, *Pinky*, *Home of the Brave*, and more. In sports, Jackie Robinson was named the National League's Most Valuable Player of 1949, a milestone that incited cheers and jeers across the country. Supporters and detractors also reacted differently to heavyweight boxing champion Joe Louis's retirement after holding his title more than a decade.

By contrast, racial disharmony continued to float at the periphery of Johnnie's personal experiences, allowing his ideals to remain intact. He saw his sports favorites as proof that any goal is attainable in American.

LOS ANGELES, HERE THEY COME

Also in 1949, Johnnie's father was promoted to manage one of the insurance firm's district sales offices in Los Angeles, where the company was headquartered. This time the family could afford to buy a home among the black elite on West 28th Street. Johnnie's mother finally realized her California dream—a spacious house with avocado and palm trees decorating the landscape and a three-car garage.

Several years later, in 1957, Hattie would come close to losing that dream. She waited too long to seek medical attention for an ailment, and her appendix ruptured before she arrived at the hospital. After emergency surgery, she hovered near death. Each day for two months, Johnnie and his sisters wondered if their mother would return home, only to hear their father's optimistic reply, "She's very sick, but we think she's going to get better."

His mother never fully recovered from the effects of peritonitis, but she resumed life at home. As one old saying goes, "God may not come when you want, but he is always on time." After her return, Johnnie vowed to spend more time with her. He stood close while she prepared dinner and admired her strength as she, without complaint, endured pain that varied in intensity but remained ever present.

3

Valuable Assets

The Cochrans flourished in Los Angeles, where Johnnie learned to manage and appreciate his personal assets. His father granted him one of many invaluable lessons when he worked to enroll Johnnie in the prestigious Los Angeles High School. Johnnie never knew how the Chief was able to get him off the path to less-desirable Dorsey High School. He did know that Los Angeles High presented big opportunities. The institution offered academic excellence comparable to a prep school and had alumni with the power and influence to prove it. Although it was a public school, many of the elite Hancock Park families sent their teens to Los Angeles High to study economics, political science, and several foreign languages, among other advanced classes. Johnnie would grow fluent in Spanish and study French and Italian there.

Johnnie started the fall term amazed by what a top educational facility could provide. Then he made himself at home on the sprawling campus, which included an Olympic-sized swimming pool, tennis courts, fencing venues, and more among the ornate brick buildings. These red buildings symbolized a plethora of possibilities and a domain in which Cochran could excel, as he always had.

CULTURAL DIFFERENCES

Despite their nicer clothes, Johnnie recognized that the students walking the pristine halls of Los Angeles High were the same as he. Joined by a handful of other blacks and Asians, he found new friends of all colors. Some friends would become future celebrities, such as actor Dustin Hoffman, while others would gain distinction in a less public limelight, like the future cardiovascular surgeon George F. Jackson, Jr.

A fair number of Cochran's friends belonged to the school's honor society. When Johnnie attended study sessions at their homes, he realized that as beautiful as the Cochran house was, the homes of his new friends were more lavish. They lived in large mansions with ornate facades and beautifully designed interior decor. Their homes were equipped with bowling alleys, pools, and other facilities for their favorite pastimes.

During this period, Cochran saw how much could be achieved. He felt at ease communing with the rich and influential and enjoyed their company without being envious. Envy represented a lack of hope for attaining similar comforts. He, to the contrary, held lofty expectations for his life and now knew that hard work could lead to a lifestyle that his parents never experienced.

For any of it to happen, hard work was crucial, whether in school or out. During high school, Johnnie held a job at the black-owned Fawn's Catering, paying 90 cents an hour. The catering business exposed him to another side of the rich. Working their parties, he observed their indifference and even disdain toward blacks and poorer Americans. When he returned as a waiter to homes he had previously entered on equal footing with his classmates, he was hardly seen as an equal. What he witnessed caused him to sympathize with workers who endured rudeness and indifference in silence because they needed a job.

He began to question the humanity of the folks who snubbed others outside their economic and racial class. To be sure, he liked the luxurious ambience of the wealthy, but he could not buy into some of their morals—or lack of morals. When sitting at dinner with classmates, for example, he said his usual prayers alone and in silence before taking a bite to eat. Some of his upbringing would not change, no matter where he was.

A TASTE OF RACISM

The job at Fawn's was not his first taste of discrimination. Direct exposure to racism had broken through the family shield earlier during visits to Shreveport. These were relaxed, fun trips until the family reached the Texas border. Crossing into Texas, his parents' apprehension heightened and the children were warned to keep quiet and stay close with no clear explanation why. At one gas station, Johnnie ignored the warnings and hopped out of the car. He headed for the bathroom, where an imposing white man wearing a cowboy hat looked down and demanded, "Boy, can't you read?" Johnnie had missed seeing the postings for separate white and black restrooms. His mother came to the confused child's rescue and ushered him away.

Although he questioned his father about the incident, racism was a sensitive subject for the proud man to discuss. The Cochrans had sheltered their children from it. Part of the conversation Johnnie recounted in *Journey to Justice* was his father's final direction to "watch and remember." Johnnie did his best to comply, but much of the devious mentality behind segregation remained a mystery. He just accepted what occurred as the way things were there. Likewise, the boy in him did not take the insults personally because, for the time being, his belief in mankind's overall goodness prevailed.

Johnnie was not immune to absorbing the prejudices of others, however. Johnnie began to avoid his first Jewish friend, Elaine Kuznitz, after reading a news article about Elaine's parents. The article called the couple "Reds" (a derogatory term for communist sympathizers) and implied that they were part of a foreign conspiracy against America during the cold war with the communist Soviet Union. Johnnie's patriotic ideals, like those of many Americans, made him susceptible to such bias. He would deeply regret that behavior later in life.

LIFE'S MISSION

Somewhere between honors classes, the debate team, quarterbacking varsity football, and holding down a part-time job, Johnnie heard about the 1954 Supreme Court ruling on *Brown v. Board of Education.* He later wrote:

> [T]he most important thing that occurred during my years at L.A. High happened miles from our tranquil campus. That May in Washington, D.C., the United States Supreme Court handed down its landmark decision in the case of *Brown v. Board of Education of Topeka, Kansas.* Legal separation with its elaborate mythology of "separate but equal" public institutions for black and whites was forever overthrown.

The decision of the Supreme Court set legal precedent on May 17, 1954. Many whites viewed the court's decision as an assault on the public school system. *Brown's* persuasive argument actually laid the foundation for ending segregation in all public venues. Citing it in *Gayle v. Browder,* the case associated with the bus boycott in Montgomery, Alabama, the court closed the door on Jim Crow laws. But *The Southern Manifesto*

Thurgood Marshall and *Brown*

Many people fought for reversal of the *Plessy v. Ferguson* decision, in which the U.S. Supreme Court had declared that distinct accommodations for whites and "the colored race" were legal as long as they were "separate but equal"; this was the guideline followed in the segregation of public schools. Harvard-educated lawyer Charles Houston and the Howard University students he trained were at the forefront of using the law for social engineering and reversing the *Plessy* ruling.

In his early work, Houston documented the disparities between black and white educational facilities for predominantly white lawmakers to compare. With this information, he was able to prove to the Supreme Court that separate was anything but equal in the case of *Missouri ex rel. Gaines v. Canada* (1938). He accomplished this with the help of former student Thurgood Marshall.

Marshall, under the auspices of the NAACP, went on to argue the cases of *Sweatt v. Painter* and *McLaurin v. Oklahoma State Regents* in front of the Supreme Court in April 1950, each of which pinpointed racial inequities at the college level. The next five related cases, after being consolidated by the court, were to topple definitively the legally sanctioned segregation in lower schools. *Briggs v. Elliott* of South Carolina, *Davis v. County School Board of Prince Edward County*, *Virgina*, *Bolling v. Sharpe*, and *Gebhart v. Belton* were all consolidated under the name that is now so famous: *Brown v. Board of Education*.

Marshall, along with his NAACP lawyers, argued the cases in front of the Supreme Court. Perhaps the most persuasive addition to their argument was evidence of psychological harm. A number of studies supported that fact, including those of Kenneth Clark and his wife, Mamie Phipps. Together these studies linked the low esteem found in black children to segregation and institutional inequities, concluding this in a way that moved the justices to action. Writing the official opinion of the court, Chief Justice Earl Warren reported that the court asked itself the question, "Does segregation of children in public schools solely on the basis of race, even though the physical facilities and other 'tangible' factors may be equal, deprive the children of the minority group of equal educational opportunities?" The court stated unequivocally: "We believe that it does."

"Like so many other African Americans, I was thrilled that the justices' opinion was unanimous, and I will revere Chief Justice Earl Warren and Justice William O. Douglas until the day I die," Cochran wrote in his first memoir. "But,

(continues)

Thurgood Marshall and *Brown (continued)*

to me, the most striking images of those exciting days in 1954 were the pictures of the tall, handsome lawyer who had argued *Brown* before the Court. He was Thurgood Marshall of the NAACP Legal Defense Fund." Cochran described Marshall as a black man like himself. "More importantly," he recalled, "he had used the law and his storied skill and courage as an advocate to change society for the better."

Declaration of Principles, recorded in Congress on March 12, 1956, and signed by 101 Congressmen, made it clear that many politicians continued to support segregation.

Adjectives like "noble" and "exciting" were applied to the legal profession after the landmark *Brown* decision. Johnnie had previously announced his intention to become a lawyer while in junior high. The career choice surprised his parents. His skeptical mother eventually came to terms with her son's decision, although the lofty professions of doctor or research scientist appealed to her more.

Before Johnnie had looked at his schoolmates' fathers and saw the comfortable lifestyle the legal profession could bring to him. After observing Thurgood Marshall, however, he realized lawyers had the power to fight injustice in American society; they could level the playing field. His legal mission became firm as he watched the civil rights movement progress. He wanted to carry on that struggle. To prepare, he read everything he could find about Marshall, his hero. Marshall fought to rectify errors and omissions in the law, advancing legal equality for black Americans. Cochran's battle would pick up where Marshall left off, putting equality into practice by forcing good social judgment through the law.

For the time being, Cochran's fighting spirit, demonstrated in his athletic pursuits and ROTC training, grew

Thurgood Marshall, pictured here in 1962, argued for the plaintiff in *Brown v. Board of Education* in front of the U.S. Supreme Court in 1954. Marshall's work inspired Johnnie Cochran to pursue a career in law.

stronger as he tackled his studies and after-school jobs. Preparation for his mission would begin in earnest following graduation and, of course, after prom night. Sometimes, even a would-be revolutionary needed fun.

HIGHER GROUND

During Johnnie's senior year of high school, another of his mother's dreams came true. She gave birth to a fourth child, a son named RaLonzo Phelectron Cochran, called "Flecky" for short. While Flecky was still nursing, Johnnie was thinking about the top university in the country. That meant Harvard to him. His father wanted nothing less for his son, but he had to send three other children to college. An Ivy League education was not affordable. Disappointed, Johnnie settled for the University of California, Los Angeles (UCLA), and saved his earnings from a summer job to cover expenses during his freshman year. His initial disappointment with UCLA evaporated once he stepped on campus. "The University of California system is one of America's great public treasures—world-class institutions of higher learning open to all, purely on merit," he once gushed.

While at UCLA, Johnnie carried a full course load in business administration on top of working part time. He was not alone in this. Studying while holding a job appeared to be a common disadvantage for minority students on campus. Johnnie got a huge boost when he teamed with Todd Reinstein and Joe Burton, who bought their textbooks in the summer for an early start on the year. They helped him get ahead on his courses and showed him how the college game was played. He enjoyed the challenges.

African Americans and Jews were excluded from the best study groups, as well as from white fraternities and sororities. These Greek chapters were more than social. They ran cram sessions. Older students tutored younger ones in coursework recently passed, using exams from previous semesters.

Johnnie pledged Kappa Alpha Psi, a large black fraternity founded in 1911, and rose to president of the chapter. He discovered added support there. Some Kappa brothers offered their fellowship for life. Older Kappa and mentor Tom Bradley, who became the first African-American mayor of Los Angeles, remained one of Cochran's friends and threw prestigious work his way. William Baker, a fellow pledge, became a decorated inspector in the Los Angeles County Sheriff's Department and married Johnnie's sister, Pearl.

DUAL LIVES

During his time at UCLA, he worked part time in his father's office selling insurance to African Americans living in the Palm Lane projects. Friday evenings in Palm Lane took on a meaning greater than money. The residents transported him back to his roots and gave him a better sense of the black struggle.

He could identify with the people in Palm Lane. They reminded him of his parents, their lengthy workdays to make ends meet, and the Southern culture they left behind in search of a dream. A better life came to his family, but Palm Lane was a long way from the easygoing gentility of West 28th Street and the academic competition of UCLA.

On Friday nights, Johnnie gassed up his used yellow-and-black Ford Fairlane convertible and directed it to the projects. Once there, he tried to catch the residents at home watching

IN HIS OWN WORDS...

Cochran's job for his father's office required him to collect insurance premiums (debits). In the memoir *Journey to Justice*, he wrote of a period of teenage reflection on his insurance clients in the Palm Lane projects:

Yet the longer I worked the Palm Lane debit, the less the difference between these families and my own seemed to matter. Listening to their stories, their hopes and disappointments, I began to discover how deep our connections to one another really were. Faith, family suffering, fortitude and our common experience of the majority community's discrimination and indifference bound us to one another as surely as iron chains had once bound together our ancestors in the reeking bellies of the slave ships that bore them out of Africa. With that realization, the voices of Palm Lane took their place in my soul, alongside those of the Little Union Baptist Church. And, as they did, the comfort I had always slipped into between my very different worlds began to fall away. For the first time in my life I felt divided and uneasy.

Friday Night Fight on television. Hospitality greeted him, and between boxing rounds his clients shared familiar stories about dreams of escaping poverty and the frustrating road-blocks that held them back. Just as relaxed here as in Hancock Park, he listened like a seasoned salesman was supposed to do. His clients' stories appealed to something deep inside him and showed how discrimination could erode every aspect of life. This was no intellectual exercise. The haunting truth was that any one of those people could have been him.

He began to recognize a dual culture in America, along with some of the attitudes that perpetuated it. Unlike many Palm Lane residents who felt defeated by racism, high expectations were engrained in him. Yet the world was a more complex and rockier place than he once believed. He saw competition at its extreme bury fairness under oppression. Coming to this realization, Cochran re-examined everything about himself, except his religious beliefs.

"I am so proud to be an American. I believe with all my heart in the words of the Constitution, but for African-Americans it is impossible to ignore the reality of racism," he observed.

His total ease with West 28th Street and UCLA vanished. He felt planted in two opposing cultures and had to wonder if his lifestyle and aspirations implied indifference to the suffering in Palm Lane, or if it might require shelving the black identity that was solidifying within him.

RECONCILING DUALITY

Cochran pursued his dividedness—this search for himself—the way he addressed any quandary: with study. He began to absorb African-American history and to learn about freedom fighters such as Frederick Douglass and the Niagara Movement, which had become the NAACP. W.E.B. DuBois, a founder of the Niagara Movement and the NAACP, was one of his favorite philosophers, in addition to other black intellectuals who wrote extensively about race. They described a sense of "two-ness" pervading the African-American community.

After much study, Cochran concluded:

> This concept of 'two-ness' is one that has eternally intrigued me. It is at the very core of the American racial dilemma. In DuBois's words, we as Americans and blacks are forever wrestling with this contradiction, which has its roots in the anguish that was slavery. We were never viewed as just teachers, doctors, lawyers, scientists, and writers. We were perceived as black teachers, black doctors, black lawyers, black scientists, and black writers. Every decision, every action we made as professionals was and still is defined by this cruel color line.

Cochran joined legions of people who felt a difference as a result of being black in America. Cochran's family handled the duality by believing their personal lives could improve and by working hard to make improvement happen.

SELF-IMPROVEMENT CONTINUED

Not everyone handled this duality through hard work. Johnnie discovered the opposite on his night shift at the post office. Clocking in at the Terminal Annex precisely at 6:06 P.M. and clocking out at 2:06 A.M. provided more money for his last year at UCLA and for law school. Sorting the late-night mail also fit his busy daytime schedule, but he was surprised to see people's different approaches to the job.

For instance, a few women clocked in, and then left with their boyfriends until it was time to clock out. One black guy had been through law school and had passed the bar. When questioned about what happened to his law career, he simply said, "[T]hings didn't work out." In addition, freely expressed UFO and political conspiracy theories served as distractions from the rest of the strange work habits. Without a doubt, Terminal Annex was a far cry from UCLA, where students were doing whatever it took to come out on top.

During this time, Johnnie met Barbara Berry, a young lady with a background similar to his. She hailed from Shreveport and had settled in Los Angeles via the San Francisco Bay Area. Her classic intelligence and ambitious street smarts helped her get into UCLA after both her parents died. Johnnie admired her strength. They began dating, despite whispers around the university that she was searching for a husband. Soon after, he shocked his friends. He purchased an engagement ring with money from a $500 Kappa scholarship, minus what he spent on books. She accepted the ring and his proposal. Then he continued working toward his career plan.

At the time, Berry seemed a better fit for Cochran than his choice in law schools. Following graduation from UCLA in 1959, he attended Loyola Law School in Los Angeles. In his opinion, "The Loyola regimen combined the brain-crunching work of a competitive graduate school with the human sensitivity of a Marine boot camp." He never liked the place. In his first year, he saw more of the campus and his study partners Merv Brody and high school friend Ron Sunderland than his fiancée.

Cochran spent a lot of time with Sunderland and his wife, Ruth. The atmosphere of their marriage felt as warm as the Cochran household. The bond forged between he and the Sunderlands would last a lifetime and serve as a model for his ideal of a happy life. By contrast, his marriage to Barbara Berry in July 1960 would eventually collide with some insurmountable obstacles.

LEGAL INSIDER

During his three years at Loyola, Cochran broke the color barrier in the Los Angeles city attorney's office. City attorneys represented the legal interests of Los Angeles and prosecuted minor crimes and misdemeanors, while leaving felony

Johnnie Cochran is pictured here in an official portrait from Loyola Law School. During his time at Loyola, Cochran was married and welcomed his first child.

offenses to the district attorney's office. Cochran became the first black law clerk in the city attorney's office and loved every minute of it.

He, in turn, was well liked by colleagues. His supervisors quickly gave him greater responsibility by allowing him to try cases in front of judges in small claims court, where lawyers cannot practice. This experience representing the city enabled him to hone legal skills in a practical manner that won more cases than it lost.

Early in 1962, before graduation in June, his first daughter, Melodie, was born. Berry took maternity leave from her teaching position. She remained at home to nurture the couple's bundle of joy. Cochran took a leave of absence from his office and studied full time with Sunderland for the California bar exam. With no money coming in, a new child in the Cochrans' lives, and family bills mounting, he told Sunderland, "I can't afford to take this thing more than once. In fact, I'm not sure how I'm going to afford taking it this time." His anxiety about the test spiraled upward.

After a car accident destroyed his old Ford Fairlane, however, his family gained anxiety-free financial stability. The $2,000 settlement carried them through the summer, with funds left for a down payment on a white Chevrolet Impala. Cochran completed his studies, took the bar exam, and returned to work to await the results.

Cochran heard that he and Sunderland passed the state bar from an overanxious colleague. Hard work paid off: They were lawyers at last.

On January 10, 1963, Cochran reported to work as a deputy city attorney. This was his time to gain legal experience, starting with traffic court. He benefited greatly from supportive colleagues, only three of whom were African American. Over the next couple of years, he participated in 125 trials by jury, in addition to numerous cases presented before judges. With each trial, his comfort in the courtroom grew, giving him the freedom to display his brand of subtle humor, particularly when cross-examining a witness in front of a jury. He developed a notable flair that kept his colleagues entertained and, often threw the defense off guard. "If you received a traffic ticket," he joked in his second memoir, "you did not want to be prosecuted by Johnnie Cochran."

4

Irreconcilable Differences

Deputy city attorney Cochran tried 30 traffic tickets in his first day and won almost all. He was elated. His winning streak extended each day until he had to admit there was more at work than his fine-tuned skills. The testimony of ticketing officers, in front of a judge or jury, became the accepted truth. Their stories from one incident to the next were very alike. Official reasons for stopping car after car and descriptions of the so-called drunken drivers they arrested sounded more like recited mantras.

"Every suspected drunk driver they stopped had provided them with an absolutely classic case of probable cause. Once stopped, every one of those defendants behaved in precisely that way and displayed precisely the symptoms required to obtain their conviction for driving under the influence of alcohol," Cochran observed.

He began to think the officers were actually the ones in the wrong, but it appeared futile to try to do anything about it.

Attacking the police was not seen as part of his job. Just the opposite; it could be a career ender. As prosecuter, Cochran said, "Cops, attorneys, courts, defendants—we all were dancing to the same music. And the tune was being orchestrated down at police headquarters." The heavy-handedness of the police landed unevenly on people of color, specifically those of Mexican and African descent.

There were also instances of undue censorship. For example, artist Wallace Berman was arrested in 1957 after an anonymous complaint led to the discovery of a small nude drawing, which was described as lewd. He was convicted of displaying pornography and given the choice of a $150 fine or 15 days in jail. Actor Dean Stockwell paid the fine to keep his friend out of lockup.

Left unchecked for years, the censorship campaign crossed racial barriers and fell on Cochran's desk. In one case, charges were levied against Lenny Bruce, one of the most controversial entertainers in the early 1960s. To the extent a misdemeanor trial can reach celebrity proportions, Cochran's prosecution of Bruce achieved those levels. Supposedly anonymous complaints about vulgarity in the comedian's stage performances led to an investigation by the sheriff's department. A detective investigated the allegations by viewing and taping Bruce's shows. He noted the liberal use of profanity, some tasteless jokes, and a few jabs directed at U.S. political leaders. Charges were filed.

Bruce arrived in court with millionaire trial attorney Syd Milton Irmas. Irmas's persona overshadowed the fairly inaudible tape presented as evidence by young Cochran. In front of a bevy of media representatives, the case was dismissed, marking a win for First Amendment freedoms over Los Angeles' obscenity law.

EYES WIDE OPEN

Something good did come from the encounter. Cochran and Irmas formed a solid friendship. The loss to Irmas had no

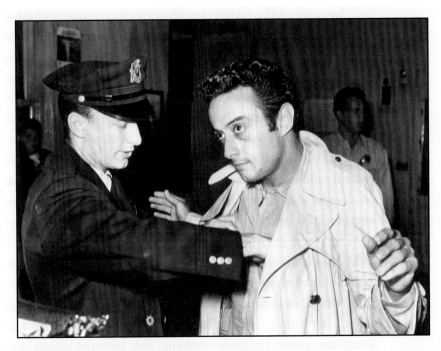

A policeman searches comedian Lenny Bruce (right) after Bruce's 1961 arrest for allegedly using obscene language during his act in a San Francisco nightclub. Johnnie Cochran acted as the prosecutor for a later case against Bruce, though it was quickly dismissed from court.

detrimental effect on Cochran's reputation in the office of the city attorney. He was becoming a top trial lawyer for the city. This priceless status brought to his desk more and more cases of police interference and resisting arrest, called Code 148 violations.

Again the police delivered similar testimony—with descriptions that were too pat—against defendants who had obviously been beaten. Police officers sat on the witness stand without a scratch while defendants hobbled to the defense table with fractured limbs or noticeable cuts and bruises. "Ninety percent or more of the defendants had something else in common: They were African-American men," Cochran said.

balanced his passion for the law with a strong sense of humor. Humor came in handy as they sat next to battered clients who were unable to win acquittals in Code 148 cases.

Nothing had changed in the system. The police operated with impunity. The best Cochran could do was strike deals with his friends in the city attorney's office, offering no-contest pleas to lesser charges of disturbing the peace. The deals freed innocent clients but justice was not truly served. The situation frustrated Cochran. It frustrated the black community, too.

The day Cochran and his family moved into the first house they owned, rioting broke out. It was August 13, 1965. They moved to the black middle-class neighborhood of Leimert Park, a safe distance from impoverished black and Latino communities in Watts, where the riots centered. Many residents in Watts did not own their own homes or the businesses in the neighborhood. They drifted economically, with their spirits in pain.

As wrong as the burning, looting, and other violence was, many in the black community understood this rebellion for what it represented. To them, it was not a question of why the community exploded. The more important issues were how had these individuals held in their frustration and rage for so long and how could they return to the old patterns of silence and denied justice.

Without question, the destruction and the deaths resulting from the riots were unjustifiable, but Cochran saw beneath the rage and reflected that "ours was a struggle to convince white Americans that we, too, were entitled to the Constitution's protections and they, too, were subject to its constraints." He acknowledged, "The burning of Watts, no matter how great the provocation—and it was great—could not advance the struggle."

Equal rights had to rise from the burning embers and blanketing smoke if there was to be lasting peace. Instead, African Americans were arrested in droves without respect to their guilt or innocence. Cochran did not know what to do

The day Cochran and his family moved into the first house they owned in California, rioting broke out in Watts. The riots were triggered by the arrest of a black man on charges of drunken driving.

about the broader issue of enfranchising marginalized blacks. What he could do was try to keep as many of them as possible out of jail.

IN DEFENSE OF THE TRUTH

In six days of rioting, 35 people died and more than 1,000 were injured. Some $200 million in property was destroyed over an expanse of 150 city blocks. The violence began with a traffic stop. Alleged strong-arm tactics by the police in the arrest of Marquette and Ronald Frye and their mother, who tried to come to her sons' rescue, triggered young onlookers to throw rocks and bricks. The LAPD responded by redoubling its efforts and uncontrolled rioting resulted. In the wake of the rebellion, almost 4,000 adults and more than 500 young people were arrested.

Cochran did not have to solicit business, for the LAPD generated more than his two-man office could handle, especially in the aftermath of the Watts riots. The police rode through black neighborhoods, stopping to line up and arrest young people as suspected felons in the riot.

He fought for the rights of those arrested late into the night. Experiencing mixed success, he returned home more frustrated than the day before, in spite of the monetary benefits. For days he entered his house exhausted, pockets bulging with more cash than most small black legal firms could imagine. One night the words of Police Chief William Parker blared from a newscast. "We're on the top, and they're on the bottom," Parker exulted. "We've got them dancing like monkeys in a cage."

A NEW DAY, A NEW WAY

Cochran's anger at the system supporting Parker's words made him resolute. "I would have to assume the responsibility of using my legal skills to change things for the better," he thought. This would be no small feat, as he well knew, having seen the system's ruthlessness from inside. He would be one man going against a Goliath; "Philistine" is the term he preferred.

Cochran decided the time had arrived to strike out on his own. He sought an office in the Union Bank Building, centrally located between Los Angeles' black and white worlds, because he envisioned serving people without respect to color. The immediate plan entailed taking on all comers, whether they had criminal, civil, or family issues; whether they needed a trial attorney or a legal advisor.

The year 1965 moved at a whirlwind pace—private practice, a new home, and now the Law Office of Johnnie L. Cochran, Jr. There was a great deal of effort required in becoming the first black tenant in this respected building.

Patty Sikora, the leasing agent's secretary, took Cochran aside after one of many rental meetings and told him that her boss did not want to muddy the building's reputation with so-called black trash.

Numerous meetings and the scouring of his financial records could not deter Cochran. He secured office 1219 after his father co-signed the lease. The doors opened to his secretary Albertine Mitchell poised behind her typewriter and telephone, both placed neatly on a TV tray. Clients flooded into his spartan quarters. The aftermath of the riots still required legal adjudication, and many of his father's insurance clients needed assistance in family court and with wills.

Cochran made it known that he practiced the law in general, not just one specialty. By not limiting himself, the young attorney hoped to make a decent living and handle a variety of cases with social significance, similar to role model Thurgood Marshall. But just as Cochran's father found when selling insurance, part of the plan floundered because people did not believe a black attorney could handle civil litigation.

The mother of one client he saved from a prison conviction came right out and said it. "I didn't think you could handle that kind of money," she said. "They say these white boys can get more money."

There it was. His clients were willing to put their lives in his hands, but not their future finances. His colleagues expressed reservations as well. The workload would be oppressive should he land a civil case. They thought he was crazy for trying to practice criminal and civil law.

He was buried in criminal defenses, even without added civil cases, and asked Nelson L. Atkins, a friend since high school, to join him full time. Atkins had also pulled a stint in the city attorney's office. This partnership eased the work load slightly. When one civil suit did come his way, Cochran made local legal history by trying two cases on the same day, running

crowded into the courtroom, while people watching at home pushed KTLA's daytime ratings to record levels. This intense coverage made the 28-year-old Cochran a local celebrity. Young black strangers approached him on the street reciting the phrase, "Mr. Cochran wants to know," and adult African Americans added, "You know, we're proud of you."

Cochran had questioned repeated violations of police procedures, gun protocol for one, and cast doubt on the autopsy reporting a debilitating .35 percent alcohol level in the victim's blood stream. Cochran believed Deadwyler would have been comatose at that level, not driving his wife to the hospital. Although the jury decision was split, the majority ruled that the death was accidental.

Cochran confers with client Barbara Deadwyler in a Los Angeles courtroom, where she gave her version of the fatal police shooting of her husband on May 24, 1966.

District Attorney Younger told a viewing audience, "We feel that criminal prosecution is not justified in this case. And, as far as our office is concerned, in the absence of further evidence or new witnesses, the case is considered closed." Younger also lauded Cochran's conduct during the inquest, for the black attorney's professional demeanor drew respect from whites as well as blacks.

The next step was a civil suit filed against the LAPD, but the plaintiffs could not breach the blue wall. They lost the case, leaving Barbara Deadwyler uncompensated for her loss. Cochran and Nelson Atkins, who actually tried the case, took the defeat hard and would never forget Barbara Deadwyler's fortitude and grace in light of the injustice. Through Cochran she expressed hope "that despite the verdict, despite what individuals may feel, we may now from this point go forward and there will be no more bloodshed, no more killing or no more disorder."

Riots over the death were averted. Cochran wrote with admiration: "She never remarried, but despite her grief, disappointments, and hardships as a single mother of four fatherless children, she has never surrendered to bitterness."

The case took four years to resolve and cost the firm tens of thousands of dollars. Although they did not achieve the desired outcome, Barbara Deadwyler and Cochran did become lasting friends. He would spend the rest of his life indirectly vindicating Deadwyler's murder by giving African Americans a voice, even in death.

BEHIND THE SCENES

Media exposure from the Deadwyler case caused another upsurge in business. The firm became Cochran, Atkins, & Evans late in 1966, after adding Irwin Evans to meet new demands. They succeeded with more cases than they lost. The practice was becoming a multiracial community force, just as Cochran had dreamed.

His marriage, however, was falling apart. He and Barbara seemed to have switched roles over the years. She, the practiced risk-taker, grew steady and predictable, favoring safe financial choices. He, sheltered in middle-class security or at least unaware of his poverty growing up, but very aware of moral obligations to the community, was willing to take calculated financial risks in pursuit of the "Philistines."

Their second daughter, Tiffany, arrived in the middle of the marital fray. The couple argued, separated, and reconciled many times. Cochran often returned to his parents' home during these separations. His parents had split opinions about their daughter-in-law. The Chief was fond of Barbara, while Hattie's attitude was less warm.

Cochran would move back in the house on West 28th Street and Hattie carried on business as usual, cooking and encouraging her son to excel. His father, on the other hand, did not refrain from criticizing Cochran's disregard for the sanctity of his lifetime commitment to marriage. The Chief wished his son were more understanding of Barbara's desires and could accommodate her wishes to smooth over the friction, instead of arguing to the point of storming out the door.

Years later, Barbara claimed a couple of instances of physical abuse. Cochran said that under no circumstances did he ever physically harm his wife, even during their heated exchanges. After returning home to her, he, in fact, tried to follow his father's advice about giving in to her when disagreements loomed. Those attempts at compromise stopped short of renewing the couple's wedded bliss.

Their separations increased in frequency. During one, Patty Sikora, the helpful secretary of Cochran's leasing agent, walked into his office seeking a divorce and custody of her children. He was experiencing similar difficulties in his marriage, he told her. A romantic affinity arose from that conversation and continued during the subsequent work on her divorce proceedings.

After the divorce was settled and their attorney-client relationship ceased, the friendship edged into dating, which apparently continued during the periods of reconciliation with Barbara, his wife. Cochran was not proud of the way he conducted his personal life at that time, particularly given the potential harm to the children.

ALL POWER TO THE PEOPLE

The world around them was changing and Cochran's volatile marriage appeared reflective of these times. Bra-burning feminism was in the air, young men made bonfires from draft cards, and a new militancy seemed to overshadow the traditional civil rights movement. Young black leaders vocalized their position against government policies that marginalized African-American communities. When they turned violent as well, the National Advisory Commission on Civil Disorders investigated the causes and reached this conclusion: "Our nation is moving toward two societies, one black, one white—separate and unequal."

Blacks already knew that. Old guard civil rights organizations refocused on building economic independence and young emerging groups stressed meeting one's own community's needs. Veterans of the Vietnam War and survivors of the hateful resistance to voter registration and other civil rights efforts in the South joined the Black Power movement in urban centers.

Those youthful organizations stressed black pride, and some urban militants called for self-defense against any incursion into their homes, just as African Americans had practiced in the South for decades. The sentiments of the Black Panthers, a national organization founded by Huey Newton and Bobby Seale, covered all of those areas.

The Black Panthers spoke against American racism and the transformation of long-standing neighborhoods. Where people of varying economic levels once lived now stood desolate mono-class enclaves. The Panthers tried to fill the gap left by vacated services. Their food and health programs offered people a better start to the day. These activities gained popularity in the black community, especially among urban youth. The organization experienced rapid growth, attracting altruists as well as thugs. Some members expressed their anger against entrenched wrongs in fiery gun-toting rhetoric that demanded the nation's attention. This bravado received the desired media attention and more.

One clear government response to black power advocates came from FBI leader J. Edgar Hoover, who directed the bureau's secret Counter Intelligence Program (COINTEL-PRO) to target African-American dissidents. The Panthers fell under the watchful eye of the same program of surveillance and infiltration that spied on the Reverend Dr. Martin Luther King, Jr.

In some instances, the FBI worked hand in hand with local law enforcement. Such was the case when teams from the Criminal Conspiracy Division of the LAPD, joined by a few FBI agents, besieged the Central Avenue headquarters of the Black Panthers' Los Angeles chapter on December 5, 1969. The FBI and LAPD wanted to bring the Panthers' militant posturing to an end.

Melvin Cotton Smith, an alleged FBI informant and provocateur, spotted the assault forces and shouted a warning to a dozen or so Panthers sleeping in their fortified headquarters. Smith was the first to open fire over sandbags in the window. Bullets flew in both directions and police tear gas was answered with Molotov cocktails. The siege continued for about five hours before the Panthers extended a white flag in surrender.

A few people on both sides suffered wounds but no one died. When the dust settled, authorities claimed they arrived in force simply to serve a misdemeanor warrant. In light of the fighting, 13 Panthers now faced more than 70 criminal charges, including conspiracy to murder police officers.

The defendants did not have the resources to hire legal counsel. So the court appointed separate attorneys to each one. Cochran was assigned to represent Willie Stafford. Because all the defendents were being tried together, Cochran had the opportunity to meet and befriend the head of the Los Angeles Black Panthers, Elmer "Geronimo" Pratt, and Sandra "Red" Pratt, his pregnant wife who was released on bail.

The police later found Sandra Pratt's body discarded on a California roadside. She had been shot and killed. Cochran remembered one police detective taking pleasure in informing Pratt about the murder of his wife and unborn child. The officer delivered the news with a smirk. Pratt held his composure, barely allowing a hint of surprise. He believed he knew who killed his family.

A schism had arisen in the Panthers, pitting the Eldridge Cleaver faction against the Huey Newton faction. Pratt held Newton supporters responsible for Red's assassination and a brawl broke out in the courtroom between defendants from both camps. In less than a minute, the judge and the prosecutors shocked Cochran by drawing guns as they backed out of the courtroom. An alarm sounded and shotgun-wielding deputy sheriffs marched into the fight. They beat the rivals as Cochran watched, appalled at the senseless violence.

IN THE HEAT OF BATTLE LIFE GOES ON

This incident was the harbinger of a long, disturbing year for Cochran. As verbal battles raged in the Panther trial, Cochran and Barbara hammered out another legal separation. In addition, his mother fell ill from intestinal blockage. She appeared to be dying, in spite of two months of hospitalization and two surgeries.

Cochran asked his friend and former classmate George Jackson for a second opinion. The cardiovascular surgeon advised Cochran to get his mother to another surgeon without delay. Hattie's chances of survival were low by the time she underwent a third surgery, yet somehow the family's prayers were answered. Hattie left the hospital after another month of recuperation.

Cochran could not let his personal problems interfere with his job. The Panther trial proceeded with the defendants in chains. It seemed to Cochran that the prosecution anticipated every move the defense made and the strategies behind every witness called. Well after the trial, he requested federal information through the Freedom of Information Act and discovered that one of his co-counsels was an FBI informant.

Despite the prosecution's advantage, a vigorous defense turned the tables. Cochran knew the importance of a strong closing. When the jurors leave for deliberation, they carry the defense attorney's last words in their minds. To win a case, those words had better instill compassion for the way the defendant was wronged by the prosecution. Summarizing where and how the prosecution's case ran afoul is critical, but couching that argument in a way that resonates with jurors is equally important.

Cochran gave the jury strong reasons to hate Melvin Smith, who had testified for the state, over his client. He pointed out that Smith had provoked the fight while the other Panthers had been sleeping peacefully. When Cochran began addressing the disrespect shown by the prosecution toward the Panthers' work in the community, the judge became so concerned about Cochran's aggressiveness that he interrupted closing statements. In a sidebar meeting, he chastised the defense attorney against "borderline tactics."

Risking contempt charges, Cochran continued to criticize the prosecution and the police. An attorney for another defendant vilified the actions of the police as excessive and tantamount to harassment. When arguments were done, the judge, who selected most of the defense attorneys, asked them to approach the bench and stated, "I'll never appoint any of you lawyers again."

IN HIS OWN WORDS...

Cochran loved the feel of debate and the art of persuasion, whether in front of a jury or simply in a high school debate, as stated in *A Lawyer's Life*:

> In high school I excelled at debate. I don't remember a single question we debated, but the questions didn't matter as I was able to take either side of almost any reasonable statement. But I do remember that incredible surge of power and satisfaction I felt when I made a strong argument and dragged people over to my side of the question.

Cochran's parents, who witnessed their son in action, were impressed by his closing remarks. They clearly showed pride in him doing his best regardless of the court's censure. The rest was in the hands of jurors.

The jury deliberated for 11 days before bringing one of the longest trials in Los Angeles history to a close in December 1971. The jury pronounced 72 "not guilty" verdicts. Stafford, Pratt, and seven other defendants were found guilty of a minor conspiracy charge to possess contraband weapons. Praise the judge had withheld from the defense attorneys was showered on the jury for the work accomplished. Cochran offered the jurors another form of congratulations: He invited them to the annual Christmas party at a restaurant he co-owned.

ANOTHER ROUND WITH THE PANTHERS

Cochran's defense of Willie Stafford so impressed Geronimo Pratt that he asked the attorney to join in defending him against first-degree murder, robbery, and assault charges from 1968. Pratt warned Cochran that the government was out to get him at all costs, even if it meant charging him with crimes he did not commit. He repeated that he had nothing to do with the murder of Caroline Olsen and the shooting of her husband, Kenneth Olsen, for which he was charged. He claimed to be at a Panther gathering that day. Panther witnesses confirmed his presence, if not for every minute at the gathering. Cochran believed in his defendant's innocence while attributing Pratt's conspiracy theories to ideologue zealotry.

The prosecution in the Pratt case had pulled together an incriminating case. So this would be an uphill battle, the kind Cochran enjoyed. Kenneth Olsen identified Pratt as his assailant and a handgun matching the caliber used in the shooting was recovered in a house frequented by Panthers.

Cochran countered the eyewitness with expert testimony about the strong likelihood of errors in cross-racial identifications. The issue of the matching gun required a leap of faith that would be easier to discredit. Rifling marks on the test bullets did not match those on bullets removed from the victims. To explain the discrepancy, the prosecution called Julius Butler, a hairdresser and former Los Angeles county sheriff's deputy whom Pratt had ousted from the Panthers. He testified that Pratt switched gun barrels and confessed to the murder and the shooting of Kenneth Olsen.

Pratt assured his attorneys that Butler's testimony was untrue. Butler did not seem credible to Cochran in light of the enmity between the two men. Pratt again cited the government as the ultimate culprit behind the lies. With the country's problems in Vietnam and other issues around the globe, Cochran could not comprehend that the government would instigate the arrest of one mouthy activist. He would later learn that the FBI COINTELPRO's Ghetto Informant Program began targeting groups, including the Black Panthers, in 1967.

Panther founder Bobby Seale recalled the breadth of local government attacks encouraged by the FBI:

> So here we were a group of young men beginning in California and, of course, by the end of 1968 in a two-year period I got an organization of 5,000 people in 45 chapters and branches scattered throughout the

United States of America. We are really at the thresh-
old of really being attacked by the power structure.
Through that next year of 1969, J. Edgar Hoover moving his agents into various cities and chapters and
branches, every Black Panther Party office was
attacked at least once in the year of 1969 and as much
as three times particularly—the one that was hit three
times was the Chicago Black Panther Party office.

During the trial, the FBI failed to disclose that its surveillance had extended to Cochran's office phone and "an informant within the defense environs." This informant was never
named. Nor was the defense informed that Kenneth Olsen, the
key witness, originally identified a man named Ronald Perkins
as the shooter. Pratt was singled out two years later from a
photo lineup that may have been unduly suggestive.

The otherwise confident Cochrann was terribly shaken
when he lost this case in 1972. Cochran had not taken Pratt's
conspiracy warnings seriously, and that hurt the defense. He
also failed to investigate thoroughly a photograph he had
offered as evidence.

Cochran simply accepted that the photo of a bearded
Pratt was taken around the time of the crimes, as the defendant's brother believed. The young man was mistaken, and
the prosecution tarnished the defense's credibility by proving
it. The picture had importance because Olsen described his
attacker as clean-shaven, unlike Pratt, who had worn a beard
for years.

Contributing to this innocent man's imprisonment was
Cochran's worst nightmare. Cochran learned some valuable
lessons from the case, but Pratt paid a high price for his attorney's education. The Panther leader felt disgusted with the
sham masquerading as a just trial. After the word *guilty* rang
out, he refused to sit in the courtroom and listen to more verdicts. The prisoner was ushered out and later reminded his

friend, "I told you, Cochran. They're going to do whatever it takes to get me."

Cochran now promised not to give up this case until Pratt was free. He would not let an innocent friend remain in jail because of his naiveté.

He wrote in his memoir, "Today, I owe Geronimo Pratt not only a debt of justice, but one of love. Together, we both have learned just how wise Dr. King was when he taught us: 'If you don't stand for something, you'll fall for anything.'" Cochran's eyes would remain squarely on his mission, and he would not allow himself to be duped again.

5

Life Happens

Leonard Deadwyler and Geronimo Pratt were individuals without great renown, and yet their cases were, for Cochran, memorable and life changing. He heard about the government intrigue surrounding the Pratt case in bits and pieces before confirming everything through declassified files. Shaken by the knowledge, anger formed beneath his devotion to justice. He felt overwhelmed and tried to control the rage in public, but the power of it gripped him and strangled hope, much as it had done to his former insurance clients in Palm Lane. He thought he understood the personal turmoil those African Americans had endured. But, he did not really feel it until now. This rage was similar to the force that invoked the Watts riots.

Carrying on as if his rage did not exist was futile. After hiding it during the day, rage nearly smothered him at night. "I sat alone with anger," he wrote, "and listened as it chanted its mesmerizing litany of injustices." To master his anger, he returned to his lifelong religious beliefs.

He leaned on his parents and the church, until once again he recognized that he had the power to direct anger "to a decent and constructive purpose." He transformed the hatred of injustice back into a love for justice and rekindled the desire not to overthrow the system, but to change it.

He threw his better self into the case of Philip Eric Johns. Johns was shot to death in his bed in 1972 after police broke into his apartment looking for a robbery suspect. The real suspect, Carl Spotsville, who had no connection to Johns, soon turned himself in to a judge.

Johns was an innocent African American sleeping at home after a hard night's work. The two police officers said they acted in self-defense, shooting Johns after he grabbed one of the officer's guns. Another officer standing at the bedroom door refuted that version of events. The rest of the system rallied to the defense of the two officers involved in the killing.

The Los Angeles police chief and mayor declared that Johns's shooting was an action taken in the line of duty and that the two men should be exonerated. Police investigators concurred. There would be no criminal charges.

Johnie Choyce wanted vindication for her son. She asked Cochran to help her. The attorney exhumed Johns's body for an independent autopsy. While prosecution and defense experts debated the reasons for the powder residue on the victim's finger and other matters, the undeniable facts were that Johns had been shot in the chest and the back and his jaw was broken. Cochran and Choyce wanted someone to pay.

A $5 million lawsuit was filed against the LAPD. Some members of the mostly white jury called the black court reporter the insulting "burr head." This was not a good sign for Cochran and Choyce. The suit took four years to come to trial and Cochran would lose another strong case. The judge threw out the jury's verdict, but the appeals court reinstated it.

BACK TO PUBLIC SERVICE

Although Cochran was still married to Barbara Berry, he continued his relationship with Patty Sikora. Their son, Jonathan, was born in 1973. Johnnie bought Sikora a house in North Hollywood and provided financial support to her and their son. Sikora even decided to change her last name to Cochran. It is unclear if Barbara Berry knew about this, but the news became public in 1978 when Berry and Cochran divorced.

Marriage complications aside, Cochran's legal practice was very successful. He earned about $300,000 a year and had comfortable offices on Wilshire Boulevard. One acknowledgement of his success came in 1977 when he was awarded the coveted Los Angeles Criminal Courts Bar Association Jerry Geisler Award, for being Criminal Trial Lawyer of the Year. Another was a job offer from Los Angeles District Attorney John Van de Kamp. Van de Kamp wanted him to fill the number three position in his office as an assistant district attorney. Among other things, he would be responsible for the Special Investigations Division (SID) over government and police corruption. This would give Cochran influence over investigations into police shootings and other complaints. He could advocate change from the inside. Van de Kamp's own opinions seemed in tune with that thinking, which would make the process easier.

The big question was: Did he want be in government service again, at an annual salary of $49,000? Friends and mentors hinted that this job experience could lead to better offers in the future. Four divisions staffed with 85 deputy district attorneys would operate directly under Cochran. Plus, the job's administrative scope extended to all 600 prosecutors. The offer was big, and he wanted to accept it. He believed the family could tighten its spending for the length of the three-year contract, but Barbara thought he was losing his mind. Just as she said when he left the city attorney's office, she repeated—ironically, as he was returning to government service—"[D]on't do this. It's a mistake." But Cochran felt good about his decision to join Van de Kamp.

ONCE MORE INTO THE BREACH

Barbara took the girls and moved out soon after. She had movers strip the home bare, even taking the refrigerator. Shock did not adequately express Cochran's emotions when he returned home from work and discovered his family was gone. At least two emotions dueled within him. He felt upset about his failed marriage but was also relieved that the household tension was over. Barbara's sudden departure simplified his life.

On this Barbara and he agreed. Their bickering had not been good for them or the children. He began his new job in January 1978 and was divorced within the year. They shared custody of the girls, and he augmented his ex-wife's teaching salary.

At work, Cochran selected Gil Garcetti to head the sensitive Special Investigations Division. Much later Garcetti would be the district attorney who opted to prosecute O.J. Simpson. Garcetti and Cochran strove to improve the police force, but change from within the police department did not come quickly or easily.

The two men above Cochran needed "a higher-than-usual standard of proof" if charges were to be filed against any police officer. To meet this standard, SID introduced the Rollout Unit, which rushed a deputy district attorney and investigator from Cochran's department to every police shooting in the county. This way SID could collect evidence and statements independent of the police officer's chain of command and possibly skirt the blue wall. The new procedures made some officers wary.

While Cochran did not believe that the police deliberately hunted down blacks to shoot them, it was clear that in an emotionally charged situation, some officers wasted no time drawing their weapons on blacks without sufficient provocation.

Cochran selected Gil Garcetti, shown above in a picture from November 2000, to head the Special Investigations Division in 1978. Many years later, Garcetti would be the district attorney who opted to prosecute O.J. Simpson.

The Rollout Unit put a new wrinkle in what could happen after an officer fired a weapon. An officer's claim that a shooting was done in the line of duty no longer constituted the main source of evidence. Independent corroboration would be sought and the SID would not ignore where that evidence led. One sheriff's deputy, rather than shoot a suspect who pulled a knife, held the man at gunpoint until backup arrived. Why had he not "dropped the scumbug," other deputies wanted to know.

"Because I don't want to be investigated by Cochran and Garcetti," was his reported response. Those words could not have sounded sweeter to Cochran's ears. His dedication to a cleaner police force was starting to have an effect. A year into his contract he received the award for Outstanding Law Enforcement Officer.

Since the Sexual Crimes Unit fell under Cochran's jurisdiction, procedures were tightened there as well. More women prosecutors were added. The unit adopted "vertical prosecution," to make trials easier on traumatized victims. With the same deputy district attorney on the case from start to finish, victims no longer had to repeat the distressing stories of their assault to varying prosecutors. Reliving their attacks may have deterred some victims from pursuing their claims.

Cochran's boss asked him to become the founding chairman of Los Angeles County's Domestic Violence Council, which made strong recommendations for handling domestic violence calls. New guidelines required police officers to inform each woman of options for protection, backed by a list of shelters and support agencies.

Seeing another community problem on the horizon, Cochran voluntarily facilitated dialogue between black police officers and black prosecutors. Their candid discussions about the roots of increasing black-on-black crime led to the creation of the Hardcore Gang Unit. For Cochran's work in this area, he was named Pioneer of Black Legal Leadership in 1979, an award bestowed by the Los Angeles Brotherhood Crusade.

Many of the people Cochran interacted with during this period became fixtures in the Los Angeles legal system. Lance Ito, who later served as judge in the Simpson trial, was one young prosecutor assigned to the new gang unit. Bill Hodgman, a prosecutor on the Simpson case, was hired into the district attorney's office by Cochran. Officer Bernard Parks, a friend from the Los Angeles Brotherhood Crusade, became police chief and later, city councilman.

AN UNFORTUNATE TRAFFIC STOP

Cochran, the third assistant district attorney, could say he kick-started some notable careers in the legal system and made his presence felt in many quarters. Unfortunately, not all patrolmen were aware of him. One day, Cochran was driving home with his children Tiffany and Jonathan in his silver Rolls Royce. They just had a blast at the weekend re-election jamboree for Van de Kamp. Cochran maintained a speed of 35 miles per hour along Sunset Boulevard, until flashing lights and the blare of a loudspeaker called for him to pull over to the curb. He complied.

One officer ordered him out of the car, with hands above his head. Cochran suspected a Code 148 arrest was looming if he gave the patrolmen the slightest excuse. He knew about "flunking the attitude test," and moved cautiously and watched what he said to keep the situation calm.

Another officer drew his gun as he walked toward the Rolls eyeing the rear passenger area. "Don't point that gun at my son," Cochran said.

The children were inside the car, crying with fear, and he could do nothing to comfort them. In response to one child pleading for their father to make the men stop, an officer laughed and sneered, "Daddy's in trouble now." The officer with the gun in his hand pulled Cochran's bag from the front seat. Cochran's badge from the district attorney's office fell out. The power shifted. This was not just another well-dressed African-American man.

The officer immediately concocted a story about thinking the car was stolen. Imaginative, but a tale hard to swallow since the "JCJR" personalized license plate was clearly evident. Cochran was again in charge and this incident would not be swept aside. The patrolmen's supervisor was ordered to the scene, and an official report was filed.

His children watched with confusion because they believed their father and the police were on the same side. Cochran had to explain, "I'm on the same side as the good police," and wanted to leave it at that. He preferred to deny knowing why they were stopped in the first place in the hope of sheltering the children from racism a little while longer. Ten-year-old Tiffany answered the question for herself: "I think it's because we're black."

The ire of John Van de Kamp and Officer Bernard Parks over this incident drew a personal apology from then-Chief Darryl Gates. Van de Kamp's anger did not compare with the mixture of feelings roiling in Cochran.

POUNDING ON THE DOOR

In 1980, Cochran's friend and client, Geronimo Pratt, was scheduled for a hearing. Cochran wrote a letter "asserting Pratt's innocence" to the Department of Corrections. He was keeping his word never to stop fighting for Pratt's freedom. The letter, submitted on his office letterhead, did not go over well with his colleagues, who were dedicated to putting criminals away. It also placed Cochran's boss in an awkward position. Van de Kamp called him to task.

Cochran held his ground and threatened to quit rather than retract his statement. To Cochran, everything else paled in comparison to the fact that Pratt had been in jail for eight years, despite his innocence. Van de Kamp dropped the matter. Others were not so quick to let it go. Someone decided to retaliate using the red tropical eel in the aquarium in Cochran's office. Cochran found the exotic creature dead on his office floor.

The incident was another sign that reform from the inside came slowly. Until change was firmly in place, he would have to compromise his ethics with silence. He would have to be loyal to the system, whether deserved or not. That uneasy feeling called "two-ness" returned. He did not want to live in this divided state. At the end of his contract, he chose the Thurgood Marshall method of social engineering over two-ness. "Sometimes," Cochran wrote, "you really do have to stand alone outside and pound on the door with both fists."

BACK TO THE MISSION

Mentor Syd Irmas suggested that Cochran join him and restart his practice frugally. Low overhead and working with Irmas were not ideas to dismiss. He took the deal.

As they got underway, another offer came from Mayor Tom Bradley. He asked Cochran to help with the expansion of Los Angeles International Airport. With the Summer Olympics coming in 1984, the airport needed to be expanded to meet the requirements of international traffic flow. Bradley envisioned going one step further, to turn Los Angeles into a gateway to the Pacific. It seemed an interesting challenge for someone who understood the airport business, but that someone was not Cochran. Bradley convinced his friend that he had the general skills to be an airport commissioner and could acquire technical knowledge from the rest of the staff.

Accepting the largely volunteer position in August 1981 introduced Cochran to global travel and the expanse of cultures around the world. It also introduced him to his future wife, Dale Mason. They met at an airport conference in Portland, Oregon. He was watching *Monday Night Football* at a party when she caught his eye. "I am a man who has always enjoyed the company of women in general, but from that first moment there was something special about this particular woman's presence—so special, in fact, that passionate football fan though I am, I can't recall who was playing that night." She was a warm, beautiful, intelligent woman with the business sense of a marketing executive. She attended the Portland conference representing Gourmet Services, an Atlanta-based airport concessionaire.

From Cochran's standpoint, his relationship with Patty Sikora had drifted into friendship. Sikora might not have agreed with that description, though. Whatever the situation, Cochran did not see anything stopping him from pursuing

Mason. He would find that they clicked on many levels, most importantly on social compassion and business.

His thoughts were not all about romance; he had learned a lot from the masterful Irmas. A vision for a new firm grew out of their legal collaboration. He wanted a legal practice with entertainment and sports law added to his criminal and civil business. Economical though they were, shared offices did not fit his expanding goals.

One case that Cochran accepted was that of Ron Settles, who had the misfortune of taking a shortcut through Signal Hill on June 2, 1981. Settles, an African-American man, was pulled over for speeding. He was arrested, and hours later, he supposedly hanged himself in his cell. The police claimed he hanged himself with a mattress cover. Public doubt rose about the story. Signal Hill was one of those places most blacks avoided because of fears about police abuse.

Settles was a young man with an up-and-coming career in professional football. Suicide made no sense to anyone who knew him. His parents, along with his football coaches and teammates at California State University at Long Beach, confirmed that he looked forward to playing pro football at the end of this, his senior year. Pro scouts, for the Dallas Cowboys and other teams, had their eyes on him. His parents did not want money for his death— they wanted their son's reputation restored. They needed reassurances that his values had not changed and that allegations, like those of drug use contributing to his arrest, were untrue.

Cochran had learned to value his own judgment through thorough investigation of the facts. He checked the Signal Hill jail and the people in it on the night Settles died. This gave him an independent picture of what had happened in Settles's jail cell. He questioned witnesses directly and presented a defense that suggested Settles had died as a result of the chokehold technique regularly taught to police officers.

Jurors thought the defense raised some interesting points and ruled Settles's death a homicide. Cochran and the original attorney for the Settles family filed a $50 million lawsuit. They had a strong case made stronger after the second autopsy, when Settles's body spoke for him. Experts on both sides of the case agreed there were no drugs. New York forensic pathologists Michael Baden and Sidney Weinberg concluded that Settles's death probably came from "a combination of carotid and bar-arm choke holds." Given the history of deaths at the Signal Hill police station and civilian eyewitness statements, the Settles family believed they had learned the truth.

Settles's mother was not well and the stress of the legal proceedings was taking its toll. She and her husband decided to end the case. Cochran was itching to bring the case before a jury, but he lived with a $760,000 settlement. It was the largest settlement from city government to date.

Mr. and Mrs. Settles harbored no ill will against Signal Hill. They just felt sorry for those who practiced such inhumanity and did not want what happened to their only son to happen to anyone else's child.

ONE MISSION ACCOMPLISHED

Van de Kamp and Garcetti closed the criminal case without prosecuting any Signal Hill police officers for murder, while the personal injury suit loomed over their heads. In that sense, the wall of silence remained, but with a crack. The media widened the crack until it exposed a pattern of deaths of people of color in Signal Hill police custody. Unable to ignore the horrendous public disclosures the county restructured the town. Cochran felt gratified as questionable leaders and complicit government personnel were replaced.

Before this settlement, Cochran had rented a spacious suite on his favorite street—Wilshire Boulevard. There, in his new offices, he received a call in 1982 from Dr. Herbert Avery, an old UCLA classmate. The call was not to refer a case, as he had done with Mrs. Deadwyler years ago. He needed help for himself this time. This successful gynecologist lived in the prestigious hillside near Cedars-Sinai Hospital, where he was on staff. Driving near his home in 1978, he noticed his son and son's friend being held in a vacant lot by the police. He stopped to help, identifying himself as the young driver's father and the car as his.

The police declined his assistance. They later said the stop was made because of a broken taillight and that the boys were pulled from the car when the driver could not produce the owner's registration. Nevertheless, the police ordered Avery out of the neighborhood in which he lived. When he failed to leave his son, an officer hit him with a police baton and placed him in a bar-arm chokehold. He was taken to jail, then subsequently released. No charges were filed against him, a technique Cochran had seen used to avoid further scrutiny of police misconduct.

Avery's treatment at the hands of the police set him reeling. At his age, being rendered powerless to racism in front of his son obliterated his secure life and the self-respect he had worked hard to build. He was unable to shake his bouts of depression, because no place felt safe. The chokehold also left him with "relentless" neck pain. He called his friend Cochran after dismissing a series of lawyers who worked on his lawsuit against the city.

Cochran plunged in and won his first million-dollar verdict—$1.3 million, in fact. They settled for $750,000 as the price for using a dangerous chokehold and doing so without cause. That same year, Los Angeles County would receive its final message on the subject.

James Mincey, Jr., was driving a 1974 Ford Pinto with a broken windshield. He accepted a ticket for the infraction and continued on to his mother's house in the San Fernando Valley. Before he got far, another patrol officer attempted to stop him.

Instead of pulling over, he sped to his mother's house and stopped in her driveway with a number of police vehicles in pursuit.

The young man struggled to reach his mother's door and was eventually subdued with a chokehold. He convulsed and lost consciousness while his mother, who had come outside, screamed for the police to stop. Following standard instruction, they maintained the pressure until Mincey ceased moving against them. He did not regain consciousness and died after two weeks in the hospital.

Cochran teamed up with the NAACP and the American Civil Liberties Union (ACLU) to fight future use of the chokehold. Mincey's killing served as an example. "This is a case about a guy who was stopped for a traffic violation and was basically given the death penalty—right in front of his mother. He didn't deserve to die," Cochran pleaded before the Los Angeles Police Commission. A lasting moratorium was placed on the chokehold technique.

FLYING HIGH

Los Angeles International Airport's Tom Bradley International Terminal opened on June 7, 1984, and provided the high-capacity infrastructure Mayor Bradley wanted for a modern port city. Cochran was proud to be a part of this achievement. He remained on the airport commission until 1993, serving as its president for three terms. During that time he won another Trial Lawyer of the Year Award, this time from the John M. Langston Bar Association. In 1984, he served as special counsel to the Democratic National Convention.

Changes were taking place in Cochran's personal life. In 1983, according to Patty Sikora, she and Cochran reached a property agreement and he promised her lifetime support. From then on, they spent less time together. Meanwhile Cochran was getting closer to Dale Mason.

Mason, who hailed from New Orleans, Louisiana, was raised in a family of means. She and Cochran courted for three years, getting to know each other and their families. She was often seen at his side at high-profile functions. During their courtship, he discovered they had much in common. Their upbringings centered on strong religious beliefs, though she was Catholic. They both had studied marketing and moved through the business world comfortably. They fit well into each other's family and life.

Cochran was in love. It took a little coaxing from his father to help him realize that. The couple was married on March 1, 1985 at the Bel Air Hotel in Hollywood. They honeymooned in Acapulco, Mexico, and continued to travel internationally throughout their marriage.

A FULL LIFE

Cochran returned to doing the job that made his mother proud: defending average people against a system that frequently failed them. Lawsuit verdicts pushed the cost of those failures higher and higher. He thought the monetary pinnacle had been scaled until the jury awarded Patty Diaz more than requested for her suffering.

Diaz, a 13-year-old girl, had been molested by a police officer who used his law enforcement status to enter her house, then returned a month later and tried to assault her again. As a result of his actions, the teen was diagnosed with post-traumatic stress disorder carrying psychotic features. She attempted suicide on three occasions. For her continuing suffering, Diaz was awarded $9.4 million plus attorney's fees, a new high for Cochran.

As if litigation was not enough, Cochran became the lawyer representative to the Ethics Committee in the 99th U.S. Congress. He eventually developed a Washington, D.C., client base large enough to sustain a law office there. In 1991, that firm became Cochran, Mitchell, & Loftkin. As his mentors had predicted, plenty of doors opened after his three years as assistant district attorney.

Johnnie Cochran is shown here with his wife, Dale Mason, arriving at London's Heathrow Airport in 1995. Cochran and Mason were married in Hollywood in 1985.

Cochran rode this winning streak in the early 1990s right into more awards and recognition from his Kappa Alpha Psi fraternity, the NAACP, and others. One award in particular, the 1990 Trial Lawyer of the Year, made him the first attorney to receive that title from the Los Angeles Trial Lawyers Association and the Los Angeles County Criminal Courts Bar Association.

Despite all of his professional success, this celebrated attorney could not forget his other hat—that of father. In 1986, he watched his daughter Tiffany at her cotillion debut. Arnelle Simpson, O.J.'s daughter, made her grand entrance into society at the same time, so the two men shared this fatherly moment. A few years later, in 1991, Cochran attended Tiffany's graduation from Pepperdine University and witnessed her start in broadcast journalism. Jonathan was heading to his father's alma mater, UCLA, and would eventually join the California Highway Patrol. Cochran's oldest daughter, Melodie, educated in engineering and computer science, was on her way to becoming CEO of a California engineering company.

Cochran's mother, however, would not live to see any more family milestones. She had been living at the seaside condo that Johnnie and Dale bought for her, pursuing her latest passion of watching the vast sea from the living room window. "Just sitting here looking at it is like a prayer," she once said. In 1991, she was rushed from her retreat to UCLA Medical Center, where she died with family members at her bedside. Cochran would visit her gravesite weekly.

BUILDING HIS PRACTICE

At this time, the underdeveloped piece in his practice, the entertainment and sports division, began to ripen. He was dealing with entertainment contracts less than he expected. More often than not, entertainers called him to pull them out of some criminal quagmire.

By the time he entered many of those cases, public opinion had convicted the celebrity. When Cochran's clients walked free, Cochran's mystique as the man who could achieve the impossible was heightened.

Perhaps no better illustration existed than the case against Todd Bridges. It appeared to be a slam-dunk: attempted murder along with attempted manslaughter and assault-with-deadly-weapons charges in a near fatal shooting. Bridges, a child actor best known for his role on the sitcom *Diff'rent Strokes*, grew into teen drug addiction. It gripped him so much that he was unable to stay away from crackhouses. The prosecution alleged that one of those forays had become a drug deal gone wrong.

When asked who fired the shots that echoed through the block, four witnesses from inside the house, including the victim, pointed their fingers at Bridges. In addition, the victim claimed Bridges stabbed him. Bridges was of no help in his defense because he was so high on cocaine that he could not recall the event or where he was at the time. For all he knew, he could have committed the crime. Even worse, he became emotionally overwrought about what was taking place and tried to starve himself to death.

This was when Cochran entered the case. He knew better than to rely on the police investigation and the materials submitted from the D.A.'s office to the defense. Cochran mounted his own investigation to find out what really happened. His search located a next-door neighbor who saw Bridges leave the house before the shots were fired. The man's companion corroborated that story.

Bridges was acquitted of attempted murder in the 1989 trial, but no verdict was reached on the other charges. The second trial, in 1990, brought acquittals on all counts. Cochran had won the unwinnable. Bridges's recovery from drugs was not immediate. He had more scrapes with the law and several attempts at sobriety before turning his life around.

More headline celebrity issues made it to Cochran's office, none bigger than Michael Jackson's. In 1993, the family of a young boy named Jordy Chandler filed suit alleging that Jackson had molested him during their friendship. When the charges were filed, the press began bombarding the public with stories questioning Jackson's lifestyle and his relationships with children. Unsure if his celebrity image would be replaced with photographs of him in handcuffs, Jackson waited in Europe to find out if he would be arrested.

After a consultation with Jackson's longtime friend Elizabeth Taylor, Johnnie Cochran agreed to be his lawyer in late 1993. Cochran called on his old friend and then-district attorney, Gil Garcetti, for assurances that he would be notified if warants were to be issued for Jackson's arrest, so that he could surrender his client without public display.

A grateful Jackson flew home and expressed his innocence directly to Cochran. The strategy focused on containing the situation as quickly as possible. The attorney for the boy's family, Larry Feldman, had a reputation as a tough negotiator, and a multimillion-dollar deal was struck. In hindsight, many people believe the settlement was bad for Jackson. Some felt it proved his guilt. Others said it made a possibly innocent man look guilty. Without a victim willing to testify, the district attorney refused to press charges and the media roar died down. Cochran achieved Jackson's desired outcome of staunching his bleeding image. Repairing the damage done would be someone else's job.

In a 1994 interview with Laura Randolph of *Ebony* magazine, Cochran said:

> I have a contract in my files right now that was offered to a young man who came to see me whose family was struggling to get by. One of the national tabloids offered him $200,000 to say anything bad about Michael Jackson. For all of us who are African-Americans, I think there's a real lesson here. If they will try to do that to Michael Jackson, they will try to do it to anyone.

About 10 years later Jackson did go to trial on similar charges from a different young man and was acquitted on all 10 felony counts on June 13, 2005. That case was probably the biggest courtroom event since the O.J. Simpson trial.

6

Dream Victory

"Do you believe in the innocence of O.J.?" was the question posed to Cochran by a participant in an online chat on April 10, 1997. His response: "Yes I do." Others had suggested Cochran really thought that Simpson was guilty of murder. Rumors of that nature persist to this day, even though Cochran denied such talk in his book, *A Lawyer's Life*. He wrote, "Only the victims and the killer or killers were there. The rest of us can only speculate—and that includes me."

Still, he made it clear that Simpson never lied to him about events surrounding the case. Every assertion investigated turned out to be true. For example, the dream team found a witness who could place Simpson's car outside his Rockingham estate at the time he said it had been there. He was home hitting golf balls before catching a flight to Chicago for a golf appearance, near the time of the murders. Also around the time of the murders, he made two attempts to reach his girlfriend, Paula Barbieri. Cell phone records verified both calls.

Several of Nicole Brown's neighbors heard one or more dogs start to bark around 10:30 P.M. One witness recalled two men arguing outside Brown's condo while the dogs howled and soon after observed a white car driving away in the opposite direction of Simpson's house. Since Simpson's limo driver confirmed seeing him at 10:55 P.M., these events would not match up with the prosecution's timeline.

Further investigation of the crime scene by the defense revealed more dents in the prosecution's case. The murder was thought to have a single perpetrator, but a second shoeprint was discovered outside Brown's house by investigators from Cochran's team. The defense's forensic specialist also concluded that Brown and Ron Goldman had fought their attackers, making the single killer theory harder to conceive.

Nicole Brown's sister took the stand for the prosecution and described Simpson as angry and brooding at his daughter's dance recital. The defense showed a video taken during the recital revealing a proud, smiling father. Outside the trial, Simpson admitted that he avoided Brown that day, not out of animosity, but because they had decided not to reconcile, and he thought it best to have as little contact as possible. He insisted they were friends who still handled parental responsibilities together. At the recital, Brown had saved him a seat with the family, which he felt demonstrated a friendship existed.

With this evidence, Cochran's dream team could poke enough holes in the prosecution's case about the timeline of the murders and the possible motive. By contrast, the blood trail, gloves, and other physical evidence were more troublesome.

After discovering the murders of Brown and Goldman, the police went to Simpson's house in search of clues. Upon arriving, they admitted, they climbed the fence to access the estate because they thought someone within needed emergency assistance. They entered the property without Simpson's consent and searched the property before a warrant was obtained. The defense argued that Simpson's Fourth Amendment protection against unreasonable search and seizure had been violated. Judge Lance Ito chided the police on their questionable excuse to make the search, but refused to throw out the evidence found there. The evidence—bloody spots, a glove, and a sock—seemed to suggest that O.J. Simpson was guilty.

As usual, Cochran would take nothing at face value, not the police or their evidence. On the dream team, lawyers Barry Scheck and Peter Neufeld were in charge of the forensic science and would make known the errors in the investigation's collection and analysis. Still, proving technical faults was not enough. If Simpson was innocent, then even wrongfully obtained evidence should not have led to him.

THE RACE CARD

Los Angeles Police Detective Mark Furhman had uncovered most of the evidence pointing to Simpson as a murder suspect. He found much of the evidence at Simpson's residence, and his testimony was very important to the prosecution's case.

From the beginning of the trial, Cochran believed that Fuhrman's weakness was racism, which may have led him to plant evidence to frame Simpson for the murder. This argument was not without its detractors. Even Robert Shapiro, a member of the defense team, seemed to side with a rising media chorus protesting the team's use of the "race card." Later, in an interview taped after closing arguments, Shapiro opined that the race card had been dealt from the bottom of the deck. The race strategy would unleash contention not only between the prosecution and the defense, but perhaps also privately, within Simpson's dream team.

The case of Geronimo Pratt was on Cochran's mind, however. He would not make the same mistake and ignore the possibility of conspiracy by authorities involved in this case. The

Police detective Mark Fuhrman is show here as he testified at the O.J. Simpson trial in 1995. Fuhrman was removed from office following the trial, when he was accused of perjury for lying during his testimony.

term "race card" was new to him and he felt it trivialized a subject that affected the lives of all Americans. He agreed with entertainer Bill Cosby, who once asked, "Who owns the deck? Who dealt the cards? What are you talking about?"

Following the prosecution's question, renowned attorney F. Lee Bailey performed the cross-examination of Fuhrman. After remarking on the unusual amount of preparation the prosecution had put into Fuhrman's testimony, Bailey launched into the accusations of racism that Fuhrman would have to refute to maintain his credibility. Bailey then took the witness through racist statements attributed to him and retraced Fuhrman's steps in the police investigation—what evidence he discovered and the opportunity he had to plant it. Bailey also began establishing motives Fuhrman might have for framing Simpson. Perhaps the detective wanted to ensure a role in this big case after being dropped from the lead investigator position. Perhaps he was enraged by the interracial nature of the Simpson family.

The deputy district attorneys argued against Bailey pursuing such matters. Rancor between deputy district attorney Marcia Clark and Bailey grew quite intense. Only Judge Ito's intervention stopped the verbal sparring.

Fuhrman continues to deny planting evidence and harboring racist motives. On the stand in March 1995, Bailey asked the detective, "I want you to assume that perhaps, since 1985 or 6, you addressed a member of the African-American race

IN HIS OWN WORDS...

Cochran had plenty to say about the "race card." He wrote in his memoir *A Lawyer's Life*:

Until this trial I don't remember ever hearing the term "race card," and in fact, I despise it. It trivializes the racial problems we have in this country. Racial intolerance isn't a card game, it's reality. It has been the single most divisive issue in this country for two centuries. At different times over 200 years it has ripped apart this country, race has been the primary factor in countless deaths, and I take the racial problems we have in America much too seriously to use race to help defend a single client.

as a nigger. Is it possible that you have forgotten that act on your part?"

Fuhrman's response, "No, it is not possible."

Just to be clear Bailey asked again, "Are you therefore saying that you have not used that word in the past 10 years, Detective Fuhrman?"

"Yes, that is what I am saying," the detective answered. Fuhrman was snared, but did not realize how badly.

THE FUHRMAN DEBACLE

While the dream team was investigating every possible hold in the prosecution's theories, one of F. Lee Bailey's researchers uncovered damning audio tapes of Fuhrman months after his testimony.

Filmmaker Laura Hart McKinny recorded interviews with Fuhrman from 1985 to 1994 as part of her background research for a film that she hoped to make about female police officers. The candid interviews with Fuhrman revealed his deeply racist views.

McKinny felt the tapes were gathered in confidence and should not be made public under any circumstances. She lived in North Carolina at that point and refused to turn the tapes over to the defense. Subpoenas were issued, and Cochran argued before a North Carolina judge to gain access to the tapes and their transcriptions. Once Cochran's team could review the tapes, they heard depictions of a police force needlessly violent. As required by the legal process, they brought the tapes to Judge Ito.

The prosecutors fought hard to keep the contents of the tapes away from jurors' ears, even though their hearts were not in it. Clark admitted as much during a sidebar with Judge Ito away from the jury's hearing. "Let me begin by saying that the content of these tapes is so repugnant and so offensive that this may well be the most difficult thing I've ever had to do as a prosecutor," she stated before voicing objections to playing the tapes.

To prevent the case from slipping away on a sea of vile words, she argued that Fuhrman's comments could be mere exaggerations or fiction to help dramatize McKinny's movie script. McKinny wanted the story to be based on real police procedures and methods of harassment. She sought out Fuhrman and other police officers to achieve that goal. Clark argued, nonetheless, that the tapes needed a separate investigation and the district attorney's office would not overlook that fact. She essentially hoped the Fuhrman tapes would be dealt with outside this particular venue.

Defense attorney Gerald Uelmen countered with his belief that the tapes were an accurate reflection of Fuhrman's behavior. But whether exaggeration or simple truth, they directly impeached Fuhrman's testimony about not using the n-word.

They clearly demonstrated that the detective lied to the court, Uelmen contended. He gave more specifics: "And in item no. 40 the reference to the building of a new precinct station or new station in division 77, that the old station should be preserved because it has the 'smell of niggers who have been beaten and died' within the premises of those walls." In another example, Uelmen related, "...he [Fuhrman] refers to spending money to keep people in Ethiopia from starving to death as being a waste of money."

Uelmen pleaded to Ito that the police code of silence mentioned on the tapes needed to be broken, that the jury should hear and read Fuhrman's words and be allowed to determine their merit. Judge Ito deemed the tapes so graphic and potentially inflammatory that he only allowed the use of two.

On September 5, 1995, the tapes were played for the jury. A small dose was all the jury needed in order to recognize that Fuhrman's words were racist and that the possibility of his planting evidence was not as far-fetched as it may have seemed earlier. If a key police investigator were caught in a lie, then the evidence he brought into the case would be clouded in doubt.

SWEET VINDICATION

"The complete tapes have still never been made available to the public," wrote Cochran. "If people were permitted to hear these tapes I feel confident Fuhrman's career would end quite abruptly and he would be forced to crawl back into his hole, never to be heard from again."

What little was heard in the courtroom and was broadcast live across the nation on Court TV vindicated years of litigation by Cochran. He later wrote:

> The Fuhrman tapes supported everything I had been saying about some members of the Los Angeles Police Department since the day Barbara Deadwyler walked into my office. After spending decades of my career fighting dishonest and corrupt police officers I finally could show the whole world a cop who willfully committed perjury in a murder trial. I felt vindicated. This was the evidence that racism was rampant inside LAPD.

The nation was left to wonder if Cochran was right about the police when Fuhrman returned to the witness stand and claimed protection against self-incrimination under the Fifth Amendment when asked if he had ever falsified police reports or if he had manufactured evidence in the Simpson case. His right not to incriminate himself was upheld. But the jurors had heard enough from the tapes to reach their own conclusions.

After closing arguments, Cochran hugged prosecutors Marcia Clark and Chris Darden in the parking garage. They had fought hard, using the style of goading common between opponents in the boxing ring or on the basketball court. But in this legal game, a man's life was at stake, and at the end of this contest, the barbs tossed between these attorneys were not taken seriously. Their egos were the least of the issue.

Cochran had a good feeling about the outcome as the judge called in the jury to announce the verdict. Once the jurors reached a decision at the end of the previous week, it only took eight minutes for them to complete and return the verdict forms.

THE VERDICT IS IN

District Attorney Gil Garcetti shared his concerns about the trial's possible outcome with former President Jimmy Carter while the president was visiting Los Angeles. Carter had followed the case and, according to Garcetti in an NPR *Weekend Edition Saturday* interview with Scott Simon, Carter told him:

> Believe me, they're coming back not guilty. Oh, I think most people have agreed that he did it, but this is payback time. And maybe you haven't seen it here, but we've seen it in the South. You and I know that many innocent black men have been convicted; many innocent black men have been hanged. No one views O.J. Simpson as a threat to their community. He's not a thug. They're going to return a verdict of not guilty. And it will be viewed as a racial verdict.

Simpson had told the dream team not to celebrate if the verdict came out as they hoped. There should be no high-fives or outbursts regardless of the outcome, for two people had died—two individuals not forgotten.

Simpson rose to face the jury.

"We, the jury, in the above entitled action, find the Defendant, Orenthal James Simpson, not guilty of the crime of murder," the foreperson announced.

Despite the warning about celebratory displays, Cochran could not resist hugging his client. Simpson was free to return to his family after more than a year of incarceration. Their battle was finally over. Simpson recently praised his dream team and, in particular, said that acquittal was doubtful "[w]ithout Johnnie running the ball[.] I don't think there's a lawyer in the world that could have run that ball. I was innocent, but he believed it."

The man with the ball gave a rousing party for about 25 people in a restaurant away from prying cameras. He celebrated in style and told himself that he would never accept another criminal case.

THE WORLD AFTER THE TRIAL OF THE CENTURY

In its balance, lives were forever changed. Participants in the trial had to redefine normal. Prosecutors Darden and Clark—losers in the case—wrote books and extended their 15 minutes of fame. Of all the people in the Simpson trial, Cochran felt Fuhrman the one most guilty of a crime. But Fuhrman got off with paying fines for committing perjury during the case, then wrote a book of his own.

Those benefiting from the trial reached further. Court TV fascinated its audience with gavel-to-gavel coverage of the trial of the century and received a much-welcomed boost in ratings. Geraldo Rivera's career was revitalized when he interviewed Patty Sikora, who dished dirt on Johnnie. Lesser-known news reporters also sped up the promotion ladder. TV movies and cottage industries emerged from the Simpson, Brown, and Goldman families' misfortune.

Cochran's ex-wife cashed in on her husband's renown with a tell-all book about her life and marriage. His daughter Tiffany, an established TV reporter, told *People Weekly*, "Boy, did my life change all of a sudden. The phone started ringing, and it hasn't stopped." Most calls were from members of the media seeking more dirt on her father. She had none and disclaimed some of her mother's and Sikora's statements.

The nation became polarized. Letters poured in either to support or threaten Simpson and Cochran. No one could have anticipated the enormity of attention the case drew. Garcetti paraphrased President Carter's prediction before the

In *A Lawyer's Life*, Johnnie Cochran described the nature of the justice system and specifically the prosecution he faced in the Simpson trial:

> The trial was to determine the guilt or innocence—and the future life—of one man, but literally hundreds of people had a substantial stake in its outcome. It was never about justice, it was always about winning.

verdict, "[U]nfortunately, there's nothing you or I or anyone else can do. It's going to be a number of years before black and white really start talking to one another again."

Simpson was ostracized by many of his neighbors and hounded by the press. For instance, after his release from jail, he tried to celebrate Nicole Brown's birthday with their children, Justin and Sydney. The kids wanted to go to their mother's grave. Because of the paparazzi trailing them, that request was delayed until the cover of darkness, when the family resorted to scaling the cemetery wall.

Simpson eventually moved to Florida with his youngest two children to establish a new life away from glaring cameras. While media intrusions lessened, the cross-country move was not sufficient to escape all unwanted attention.

Some police officers were none too happy with Cochran. One Los Angeles officer approached him some time after the Simpson trial to ask if he had to humiliate the force. Cochran replied, "My brother, I did not embarrass you or anyone in the department. You humiliated yourselves."

A sector of the police force and of the nation gained some measure of relief when Simpson lost the civil suit brought against him for the deaths of Brown and Goldman by the victims' fathers. Cochran was not part of that defense—time and other commitments did not allow it. As he watched from the sidelines, the trial venue changed and a predominately white jury was assembled. Cochran knew victory for Simpson would be an uphill fight, considering the venue and the exclusion of Fuhrman.

Garcetti attributed victory substantially to the discovery of photos of Simpson wearing the Bruno Magli shoes believed to be the same make as one set of shoeprints found at the crime scene. Simpson said he was unfamiliar with the pictures and the shoes depicted and questioned the accuracy of his image in the photos from the waist down.

It was white female juror 341, the oldest in the jury, who doubted Simpson's guilt. But in a civil trial, the majority rules and the absence of doubt is not required. Unlike criminal proceedings, jurors can vote against the defendant with just a reasonable belief in his liability or guilt. The Browns and Goldmans were awarded $12.5 million each.

COCHRAN AFTER SIMPSON

Even during the Simpson trial, Cochran's world in 1995 was not entirely about O.J. He launched Cochran Consulting International to help companies that wanted to conduct business in South Africa. He wrote his first autobiography. Also that year, Academy Award-winning actor Denzel Washington dropped by to study Cochran and model his character in the movie *Philadelphia* after the lawyer who took underdog cases and achieved victory.

There were a few blemishes on this phenomenal period of celebrity. His autobiography *Journey to Justice* no doubt helped with image control after Barbara's book, *Life After Johnnie Cochran: Why I Left the Sweetest-Talking, Most Successful Black Lawyer in L.A.,* hit the stores. Patty Sikora claimed his promised financial support stopped after her interview with Geraldo Rivera. Barbara reportedly offered Patty some encouraging words for doing the gutsy interview. Cochran provided a brief rebuttal in his book.

One persistent former client began picketing Cochran's Los Angeles office after the Simpson trial and solicited others to join him. Cochran supposedly backed out of Ulysses Tory's 1983 civil suit stemming from a police shooting. Tory wanted $10 million, but it would be many years before Cochran asked for that level of compensation. He also tended toward clients more interested in justice than money. A report on the lawsuit said Tory offered to stop picketing if Cochran paid him $15,000 he was supposedly owed. Cochran got an injunction to silence Tory from alleged defamation and invasion of privacy. Tory appealed on the basis of freedom of speech and went to the Supreme Court in 2005.

Those situations represent the downside of fame. Most of this period, though, was exciting. Cochran, who wanted to slow down, began receiving calls from across the nation. Some of the calls were requests for TV appearances. The rhyming attorney had become a favorite target for comedians. Their jokes linked the phrase for the infamous gloves to all kinds of things that might not fit. Cochran could have just waited for the media circus to move on, but some of the jokes were quite funny and he decided to play along. Besides, this seemed a fun approach to retirement. He enjoyed a rhyme or two on *The Hughleys* and *Roseanne*, and waltzed onto the *Guiding Light* soap opera set. He was interviewed on the inaugural episode of the *Chris Rock Show* as well as on respected morning and evening news programs.

Instead of getting upset about the ribbing he received, Cochran went along and poked a little fun at himself. He, of course, was underestimating how much people had been touched by the Simpson trial. He had entered their living rooms day after day, becoming a main topic of their conversations—something people would not forget.

Cochran had yet to realize the true power and monetary rewards of fame. From Cochran's perspective, he had not changed as a man. Therefore, he was slow to capitalize on the hype. Others, more astute in the world of fame, looked at him and saw a goldmine.

Steve Brill, the founder of Court TV, sat Cochran next to the station's conservative analyst, attorney Nancy Grace, at the station's fifth-anniversary party. If he wanted to see a heated debate, he did not have to wait long.

Thinking those sparks would work well on television, he offered Cochran and Grace a show. Cochran had turned down other offers for TV series with him in the courtroom. Unlike those, Brill's concept gave him a forum to be himself and talk to the public about justice as he saw it. He signed a three-year contract for several million dollars. Since the contract did not preclude him from practicing law, life became bicoastal—the TV show in New York and his law practice in California.

Cochran & Grace aired as planned, but the sparks never flew. After getting to know each other, the two hosts discovered they were not as much at odds about the letter of the law as expected. Producers asked them to heat up their discourse, to exaggerate if necessary, but Cochran could hardly be theatrical about something as important as the legal system. He did take voice lessons to learn to "breathe from the diaphragm and modulate his passion."

Soon Time Warner bought the network, staff members were replaced, and Nancy Grace went back to Court TV's trial coverage. The talk show evolved into *Cochran and Co.,* with Cochran hosting guests from all points on the political spectrum. He was paired with co-host Rikki Klieman for a while as the show's ratings continued to slide. The last 139 shows were cut to a half-hour format and became *Johnnie Cochran Tonight,* which he hosted solo. This demanding pace, between the Court TV studio in New York and his family and law practice in Los Angeles, looked nothing like a transition into retirement.

Plans for retirement waned because he loved how his life was evolving. To reduce wear and tear on his body, the family relocated to New York. He kept his Los Angeles residence and,

Cochran looks over his notes before appearing on Court TV's *Cochran & Grace* with commentator Nancy Grace. The show began in 1997 and evolved over the next few years before it was cancelled.

added a Manhattan condo near Carnegie Hall. Inspired by cries for help from New Yorkers—namely, Abner Louima and the family of Amadou Diallo—he decided to expand his California law office to the East Coast. He could accomplish in New York what he had in Los Angeles, using fees from adjudicating cases for wealthy clients to finance representation for the average person—the "No Js" as he fondly called them—who had been wronged.

"It is very difficult for a poor man to get a fair trial in this country, very difficult. There is little question that O.J. Simpson would have been convicted if he were not a wealthy man," he wrote. In the criminal trial, the government spent $10 million. Simpson had to match the people's case, which included at least nine in-court prosecutors, 488 exhibits, 72 witnesses, and the resources of the county, state, and federal authorities. He matched them with a minimum of 11 in-court defense attorneys, 369 exhibits, 54 witnesses, a legal support group, and private investigative teams. Legal victories do not come easy or cheap. As Cochran often said, "You are innocent until proven broke."

7

No Stopping Now

"See, see how little she knows about me. She doesn't know about all those whom we call 'No Js' that I represent," Cochran told reporters as he and Nancy Grace promoted the launch of their TV show. Most Americans, more than likely, shared Grace's image of Cochran as attorney to the stars. Celebrity clients certainly kept him in the limelight, but by no means did they constitute the heart of his practice, which showed no signs of slowing down.

BLESSED FREEDOM

In 1997, Cochran scored a long-sought victory. The innocent friend that he had pledged his life to free walked out of prison after 27 years. Through all the celebrity clients and his own growing renown, Cochran did not forget the cause of Black Panther Elmer "Geronimo" Pratt.

Cochran convinced the court in 1997 that the outcome of Pratt's original trial was severely influenced by government surveillance on him, as defense counsel, and by the testimony of a government informant and that both critical facts remained hidden from him during the original defense. Cochran was jubilant; he called this victory "the happiest day of my life practicing law." No doubt Pratt echoed similar excitement as he emerged into the world beyond prison walls.

Cochran had given much in this decades-long fight, and he never wanted to go through that degree of professional agony again. Going forward, he would devote his attention to liability suits.

NEXT STOP: NYPD AND THE LOUIMA CASE

Between fighting in California for Pratt and hustling to the TV studio in Manhattan, Cochran saw very little of the other New York City boroughs. He did notice that New York had gained a reputation for model policing similar to the former image of Los Angeles. Mayor Rudolph Giuliani, admired by Americans after the September 11, 2001, terrorist attacks at the World Trade Center, conjured the opposite feeling in the black community, even after that tragic day. Many blacks felt his tough-on-crime policies were irrationally applied to them. They believed that "driving while black" and "walking while black" could lead to undeserved attacks by the New York police.

In the case of Abner Louima, he was "standing while black" and wearing a vest. That is all it took for the police to mistake him for a man who had punched an officer during a squabble outside a Haitian-American nightspot. Louima walked out of Club Rendez-Vous and stood to the side while watching the police trying to control a brawl. During the scuffle, one black man wearing a vest hit Officer Justin Volpe before blending into the unruly crowd. Louima, also sporting a vest, was soon handcuffed and taken into custody for assaulting the officer and resisting arrest.

Cochran converses with his former client Abner Louima. Cochran led this civil case to victory, ensuring that the police officers involved in assaulting Louima served jail time. He also negotiated a financial settlement with the police union and New York City.

Arresting officers Charles Schwarz and Thomas Wiese put Louima in the back of their squad car and carried him off. They stopped before reaching the 70th Precinct. They were joined by Officers Thomas Bruder and Justin Volpe, and Volpe identified Louima as the man who hit him. A beating ensued.

The assault resumed in a bathroom at the 70th Precinct, where Louima was taken while still handcuffed. A wooden handle from a toilet plunger was used to inflict internal damage so severe that it tore a hole in Louima's colon and damaged his bladder. He was kicked while lying on the floor in pain before being dragged through the station with his pants and underwear down around his ankles. The police then left him in a cell, bleeding.

Cochran wrote that Volpe held up the bloody stick and boasted to fellow officers, "I had to break a man tonight." He spoke as if these were still the days when slave breakers, overseers, and slave patrols were considered worthy professions.

The EMS unit arrived about an hour and a half after that. Its emergency technicians administered medical treatment and eventually transported Louima to Coney Island Hospital. The police informed hospital staff that their prisoner's injuries came from consensual sex. The coverup had begun.

Nurse Magalie Laurent knew the police explanation was not plausible and called NYPD Internal Affairs. When the police were unresponsive, she called Louima's family and shared her conclusion that he suffered from police brutality.

TAKING NOTICE

The family tried to get news reporters to listen, but none showed interest until an unidentified officer or EMS technician phoned *The Daily News* with the story. Columnist Mike McAlary won a Pulitzer Prize for his investigative piece. Because of McAlary, Louima's vicious treatment garnered national attention.

Mayor Giuliani, who usually stood up for his police force in public, found the abuse too heinous to discount. New Yorkers of all colors were outraged, and about 7,000 staged a march on City Hall in protest. To appease his constituents, the mayor appointed a special commission to review the situation. A year later, he ignored many of the recommendations coming from that committee.

Days passed before the police union would allow the four officers involved in the abuse to answer any questions. The delay gave them time to coordinate their stories. Telephone records showed unusual activity between some of the men during that period. This 48-hour rule was supposed to apply to administrative investigations, such as those conducted by Internal Affairs. It should not have been tolerated in a criminal investigation.

Two weeks after the assault, intermediaries on behalf of Louima contacted Cochran's office in Los Angeles. This was a case that could put the New York police to the test, depending on what Louima had to say. Cochran went to the hospital with Peter Neufeld and Barry Scheck. The Louima family was there for support. A weak Abner Louima told the attorneys how he was victimized and how he wanted to stop such treatment from occurring again. So did Cochran.

FIRST NEW YORK CASE

Once more, Cochran entered the picture with other lawyers already on the case. Another colleague joined the group and the legal preparation began. The case was Cochran's first in New York. He followed the steps that had proved so successful in California. He got to know the people involved in the case, including as many witnesses as could be found. He investigated the crime scene and all evidence independently.

This approach is expensive and demanding, with no guarantee of a favorable outcome. Law firms generally pay all upfront bills and do not receive any money unless a case is won or a legal fund is established. The legal team assumed much of the financial risk in Louima's lawsuit, while sparing no expenses in proving his case.

Cochran practiced law not just for the rich. He wanted to rectify certain wrongs, to use the legal system for social advocacy. That is why he accepted cases like Louima's, which flagged the changes needed. The original two attorneys on the case resigned from the lawsuit, and Cochran pressed on. He and the team had concerns about the city's objectivity in prosecuting the criminal case. He asked the U.S. Department of Justice to prosecute the NYPD officers and then backed up that request with a community lobbying effort.

When the Justice Department accepted the case, Cochran shared his investigative findings and encouraged witnesses to cooperate. He had combed the city to interview relevant parties and reconstruct events that occurred before, during, and after the crime. Evidence against the police officers was piling up. One of the most curious statements came through Tommy Wiese's attorney. Wiese relayed a version of alleged events that wove a protective picture of his and Schwarz's roles in the assaults. But when criminal proceedings came around, Wiese returned to denial mode. His defense challenged the accuracy of his confession as summarized by the Cochran team. Wiese held strong to his denials.

Officer Volpe pled guilty following a few weeks of witnesses pointing their fingers at him, and he was sentenced to 30 years in prison. He implicated Wiese and Schwarz in his confession. Schwarz, who was thought to have held Louima down in the bathroom, received a conviction that carried a 15-year, 8-month sentence, and was ordered to make restitution to the victim in the amount of $277,495. Wiese and Bruder were acquitted of assault.

Schwarz, Wiese, and Bruder were also tried and convicted on conspiracy to cover up the crime. Wiese and Bruder each received a five-year prison sentence. Both of Schwarz's guilty verdicts were overturned in 2002 because his attorney also represented the police union. He was released from jail.

THE CITY AND POLICE UNION ON TRIAL

Louima's civil lawsuit for $155 million moved forward on a parallel track. "Our job as personal injury lawyers is to get as much money as we can for our client," Cochran wrote. "I'm not the slightest bit embarrassed to write those words. People who do the wrong thing should pay for it, and the more they pay the more certain it is that they won't do it again."

The message had to be clear that brutalizing suspects and obstructing the investigation of such crimes would not be tolerated. In Cochran's mind, the police union, the Patrolman's Benevolent Association, should be made accountable for its role in the coverup, along with holding the city responsible for the totality of the crime. Attacking the union in this manner was a novel action about which Cochran had no reservation. Breaking new ground was not a problem for him when the public good was at risk.

The police union resisted more than the city. "They wouldn't even discuss discussing an offer," according to Cochran. Yet, he was sure the posturing would change. Despite years of stonewalling, the union and the city did offer a joint $8.75 million settlement, the most money ever offered to a victim by the city for police brutality. It was declined until the defendants agreed to implement meaningful changes in law enforcement practices.

When an agreement was finally reached, Louima announced to reporters, "Since that day almost four years ago I have vowed to do everything I can to ensure that the torture and cover-up I suffered will not be inflicted on my children or anyone else's children in the future."

At the same time as the Louima negotiations, several changes were made. A civilian panel to prosecute police brutality replaced the NYPD version. The level of training on the use of force was raised. The union agreed to provide police officers independent counsel. When the union would not budge on the 48-hour rule, the city agreed to exclude it from future contracts.

From Cochran's perspective, "These reforms didn't hurt the police department at all; in fact they made the job easier for the good cops." The city had lost considerable goodwill in light of the Louima scandal, and more in a subsequent scandal involving the police shooting of Amadou Diallo, a young unarmed African immigrant. The seamier side of the NYPD had grabbed front stage. These reforms that gave New York citizens a new voice helped restore some public confidence in their police force.

The settlement was completed, yet it did not end Cochran's interest in Louima's welfare. He worked with Louima and several advisors to protect his client from financial predators and unsound investments. Cochran felt a responsibility to secure Louima's financial future as he did with all clients in need of money-management help.

A NEW HOME

Before this case, Los Angeles was the only place that felt like home to Cochran. New York was an enigma without a network of people he knew or geography he understood how to traverse. "The Louima case enabled me to learn about New York City," he reflected.

Cochran made significant inroads. He learned his way around the city and the political and social fabric holding the culture together. He liked what he saw. New York had vibrant communities and active community leaders, like the Reverend Al Sharpton, who later campaigned for the Democratic presidential nomination. Cochran had found another home in which to advance his mission. What is more, he at last realized the financial weight his named carried. The Cochran Firm added a New York office that preceded the firm's explosion into a national presence.

8

The Cochran Firm in Action

"I never thought I would be in this position ever," Cochran said in a 2002 interview. Much of the credit for the unprecedented growth of the Cochran Firm goes to senior partner Keith Givens. Cochran had offices in Los Angeles and Washington, D.C., before making Givens's acquaintance. While some firms were cutting back in 1997, the Cochran firm, through Givens's skilled negotiations, expanded to 12 offices stretching across the United States.

"My career has been kind of unusual," Cochran explained. "I saw a need and I've been trying to do it, and so far it's been working pretty well. We merged with some very prominent African-American firms and a white firm in New York. So it doesn't matter the race so much as the firms who can do the business."

These mergers, expansions, and partnerships started with a chance meeting at one of Cochran's book signings for *Jour-*

ney to Justice. Jock Smith, partner to Sam Cherry and Keith Givens in Atlanta, Georgia, spoke about his group's dream, which was much like Cochran's. They wanted to build a racially diverse law firm, focusing on socially relevant cases, with first class law services provided to U.S. residents regardless of their ability to pay. Nothing formal came out of the discussion other than a desire for additional exploration.

Givens joined in the next discussions at the New Orleans Jazz Festival. They, too, ended with an informal commitment to find ways of expanding Cochran's Los Angeles office. That opportunity arrived with a disastrous accident in New York. An ambulance speeding through a red light collided with a car carrying a mother and four children. Cochran and Barry Scheck represented the mother, while the firm of Schneider, Kleinick, Weitz, Damashek, and Shoot represented the one surviving child and the woman's ex-husband.

Givens parlayed a growing adversarial relationship between the two firms into a working partnership. Givens happened to be in New York City and Cochran asked him to intercede and quell the competitiveness building between Scheck and Phil Damashek. Givens accomplished that by returning everyone's focus to the welfare of the injured parties and away from personality clashes.

In the course of his friendly exchange with Damashek, Givens discussed Cochran's growth plans for civil litigation in New York. Damashek immediately identified with the goals. He also told Nina Burleigh for *New York* magazine about Cochran, "He's a magnet for business." The Cochran Firm merged with one of the top New York firms and Given's operations in Atlanta in a matter of months in 1997, and took the vision of litigating major individual and class lawsuits countrywide.

With the ability to draw on extensive resources in New York and the other offices, Cochran could step back from information collection and dedicate his time to strategy, the part of a legal suit he loved as much as working the courtroom.

A LIFE TAKEN TOO SOON

Amid Cochran's business success, personal tragedy struck. Cochran's younger brother, Flecky, was a drug addict. He often ended up in dangerous situations. One day in 1998, he was walking away from a dispute when he was shot in the back. The killer was arrested for first-degree murder. Cochran and his father, two family patriarchs, opposed capital punishment. Cochran and the Chief's consciences dictated that they ask the district attorney to take the death penalty off the table. He complied. After being found guilty, the killer received a sentence of 75 years to life. "[F]or some people, life in a cage is the appropriate penalty," Cochran related in his second memoir. "And as far as I know, he spent the rest of his life behind bars." In true family fashion, the Cochrans accepted the grief and lived on with their convictions intact.

There were more fallen lives demanding justice. The Diallo case came to him in 1999 the way many cases do—by referral. In this instance, Al Sharpton brought him to a group meeting with the Diallo family. "I was comforted to see Johnnie Cochran was one of them," wrote Amadou's mother, Kadiatou Diallo, in *My Heart Will Cross This Ocean*. "I knew about him from having watched occasional news about the O.J. Simpson trial while I was in Bangkok." To her, he held celebrity status and was an American legal force.

That meeting unfortunately disintegrated into arguments with her ex-husband over attorneys and who would manage a financial estate that was yet to exist. They expected the money to come from people who wanted to see justice done. News reports of Amadou Diallo dying in a hail of 41 bullets reached coast to coast. Community protests against the actions of the police kept the story in the news, although portions of the news coverage seemed strange to Mrs. Diallo.

Mrs. Diallo did not recognize the press descriptions of her son as an African immigrant and street vendor. She knew a son who had watched over his three younger brothers and one younger sister while trying to fill the shoes of an estranged father. In Diallo's short life, he had experienced the world. He had lived in Guinea (his homeland), Liberia, Togo, Thailand, and Singapore, and traveled throughout Europe; but he loved everything American. He was thrilled to be in New York City, home of the Knicks. He came seeking a college education in computer science but discovered the road to college required more than a glorious dream. He needed a significant amount of money for tuition.

Ever the optimist, Diallo was convinced he could make his dreams a reality. Being fluent in English, as well as five other languages, finding a job he had no problem. What came after proved harder. Processing computer orders at Metro Group

Protesters and New York police square off on February 26, 2000, along Fifth Avenue in Manhattan. Thousands of protesters turned out to decry the acquittal of the four police officers in the shooting death of Amadou Diallo.

USA stirred his interest. It was the other part of the job, loading computers onto delivery vans, that made his back shoot pain. He was slight of build, and heavy lifting did not grow tolerable with time. So, he took a pay cut to man a merchandise table outside a shop on 14th Street in Manhattan, where the storeowner and he shared in the proceeds.

Outside that shop, Diallo became part of the city—making friends and helping regular customers. He worked hard, lived frugally with others from Africa, and saved for college. Yet he willingly delayed his personal goals to help friends in need. He gave Mamadou Alfa Diallo, no relation, $1,000 to secure a larger apartment for his growing family. A student with a tax shortfall benefited when Diallo made up the difference. Even with this generosity to acquaintances, Diallo told his mother five days before his death, "I have saved enough money for school. I am thinking I can start next year. All I need is your blessing." He had saved $9,000.

On February 4, 1999, he entered the outer door of his apartment building at 1157 Wheeler Avenue in the Bronx. A tiny glass vestibule housed the inner security door. As he paused in front of this second entrance, four plainclothes officers from the NYPD Street Crimes Unit jumped from an unmarked red car. Two officers ran up the steps to the vestibule. A third cop stood on the sidewalk and the fourth remained on the street by the car. The unit had been searching for a serial rapist and responded to a tip that someone suspicious was lurking in front of Diallo's building.

The area was shrouded in night and the vestibule was dimly lit. According to police, one of the front-line officers shouted, "Gun!" The officer nearest him reacted with several shots, then slipped and fell as he retreated. Thinking their partner had been shot, the other policemen fired their semi-automatic weapons. In less than eight seconds, 41 rounds made their way toward the glass enclosure. Diallo lay dead after the guns were silenced. The young victim lay unarmed. A wallet and a pager were found in his possession, but no gun.

COCHRAN NOT GOOD ENOUGH

More than 1,200 people were arrested in a few weeks of protests against the shooting. Cochran joined the fight so as not to let Amadou Diallo's death be in vain. The lawyer's favorite private investigator, former police officer Kevin Hinkson, was also on the case. Some people were more willing to talk to this soft-spoken bear of a New Yorker than the police. An independent story emerged that raised doubts about any officer falling backward during the shooting, and additional findings from an independent autopsy suggested bullets continued to pierce Diallo's body while he lay incapacitated on the ground.

The Diallo family probably did not understand how slowly the American justice system worked. Civil suits moved at a snail's pace for years with just the occasional flurry of activity. Always on the go, Cochran focused on other cases during the lulls. Unlike with the Louima suit, he now had a New York staff in the Woolworth Building to keep him abreast of details in the Diallo lawsuit and all of his East Coast cases.

Unfortunately, Mrs. Kadiatou, Amadou's mother, Diallo wanted Cochran to be her sole point of contact. This was not surprising to the attorney, whose clients often asked for his undivided attention. At one point, it took Mrs. Diallo more than 24 hours to reach him. Cochran explained, "I had another client I had to see in Los Angeles." He recalled her responding, "You shouldn't have other clients; you should just have this one client."

Although Cochran understood the anxiety clients feel about their cases, he had no way of knowing the cultural history involving male domination that affected Mrs. Diallo's reaction to the men around her. It was with this frame of reference that she questioned if Cochran was neglecting her

IN HIS OWN WORDS...

Cochran believed in the Diallo case for what it represented in our society. He wrote in _A Lawyer's Life_:

I understand the scenario; these officers didn't leave the precinct that night planning to kill a black man, this wasn't Mississippi in 1967. This wasn't premeditated. They didn't get out of their unmarked car intending to shoot him. I understand that police officers are frightened and often overreact; I really do understand that. I am fully aware of the reasons for that. I can rationalize and even justify that fear.

But I know one other thing; Amadou Diallo is dead, he shouldn't be dead, and if he weren't black he wouldn't be dead. I believe that with all my heart.

because she was a woman. They had only spoken two or three times. Some action was taken on the case without prior notification, she said, and updates came too sparingly for her to feel a part of the decision-making process.

In her memoirs, she added that the last straw came when Cochran suggested she return to Africa until the trial began. "Rightly or not," she said, "I felt I had been waved away, dismissed as the bush girl who should just go back to the wilds."

She decided instead to go her way without Cochran's assistance. "It was a very difficult decision, because I am proud of Johnnie, this African-American lawyer," she stated in a 2003 interview. Cochran's dismissal from the case arrived in a gracious letter explaining her concerns and that she had retained a new attorney.

Being fired from a case was outside Cochran's normal experience. It was a first. "And admittedly, my pride was hurt," he wrote, "I didn't like it, I didn't agree with the reasoning, but I understood and accepted it."

Meanwhile, the criminal case against the four officers who killed Diallo shifted from the Bronx to an Albany, New York, court, where citizens could not see the vestibule in which

Diallo's life had been taken. In Albany, the strain between the city police and the Bronx's racially diverse communities rested outside their comprehension.

Cochran recognized the legal maneuver of shifting the trial to Albany. "We fight that all the time," he acknowledged.

> That's not through happenstance cause they know. They want to get it to an all-white area where people will be, maybe, more sensitive to the police and that's not right. I think the jury panel should reflect what society looks like. You know, it should have people who understand what really happens in life, not a bunch of people who want to go be supportive of the police regardless of the evidence.

Although Cochran believed race was at the heart of the shooting, no one made it a focal point in the criminal trial. After the jury returned with a "not guilty" verdict on all the charges, the four men were free to go.

Mrs. Diallo concluded that the justice system failed her in every way. "I am not bitter," she has since said. "It is my faith, Amadou's life and death has a larger purpose." This young man with big American dreams died at age 23. She worked to give meaning to his life by joining the battle against police violence and racial profiling, and became an advocate for residency requirements for New York City police.

Cochran talked with her at various events involving social justice. He got the impression from his former client that she wished he still represented her, and so did he. He would have loved exposing the details of that February night to a jury.

HIS DAY IN COURT

He would not see the inside of a courtroom in the Diallo trial, but the Cochran Firm did file a lawsuit against Mayor Giuliani, Police Commissioner Bernard Kerik, and the

Cochran stands with Marie Rose Dorismond, the mother of police shooting victim Patrick Dorismond. The Cochran Firm sued New York City for $100 million in restitution for Dorismond's wrongful death, violation of civil rights, and pain and suffering.

undercover officer who shot and killed Patrick Dorismond about a month after Diallo in March 1999. The 26-year-old Haitian-American father of two girls had outgrown his teenage brushes with the law. He had a job as a security guard with aspirations to join the NYPD, the same force behind the Operation Condor drug sting that led to his death.

An undercover narcotics officer solicited Dorismond after he left a Manhattan bar. Dorismond declined the purchase. When the officer did not relent, an argument followed and drew in two other plainclothes officers. One officer's gun discharged during the heated argument and another citizen lay dead.

The firm asked for $100 million in restitution for violation of Dorismond's civil rights, wrongful death, and pain and suffering. There were more like Dorismond who needed the firm's strident voice nationwide. The organization would grow to have more than one 125 attorneys ready to be that voice. It would become one of the largest and most successful plaintiff firms in the country.

9

A Promise Broken

The Cochran Firm was busy in 1999. Near the end of that year's flurry, Cochran broke the promise he made with himself not to defend another criminal case. He signed up to defend rap mogul Sean "Puffy" Combs against criminal weapons and bribery charges.

Cochran had become close friends with the multi-millionaire businessman and rapper after helping him negotiate a deal on an assault charge earlier that year. The young man liked and trusted "Uncle Johnnie," as he called Cochran. Cochran had helped a few rappers, Tupac Shakur and Snoop Dogg among them, fight criminal charges. The lawyer doubled as a father figure for several of these urban hip-hop icons, and Combs fell in that group. He had asked for all of Cochran's contact numbers when his assault case was resolved earlier in the year, and Uncle Johnnie provided them, with a caution to use the numbers wisely.

Cochran was enjoying post-Christmas cheer in Los Angeles with his family when a lawyer called him for advice in a new criminal matter. Cochran offered the caller the best guidance possible—don't let his client talk to the grand jury or anyone other than his attorneys.

Similar to the Simpson case, news reporters were alerted to Combs' arrest soon after he reached the police station. Also similar to the Simpson case, Combs's New York attorney underestimated the strength of the prosecution. He let his client testify before the grand jury at Combs's insistence. The testimony disintegrated into a ruinous venture. Combs was indicted on four counts of gun charges; a fifth charge of bribery was added later on.

The indictment was part of a buckshot pattern then in vogue: spray out a range of charges and see if the defendant falls. "Especially if you have somebody with a high profile like Puffy Combs. A regular gun charge could have been a misdemeanor that could be over within a minute," Cochran reflected a few years later. Cochran added:

> He always maintained he was innocent. In this case, Jesus, by the time we'd finished they added all the gun charges, all felonies, each carrying like five years or whatever, and bribery on top of that. It was awful. It took five weeks to try that case. I could just see what was happening in that case. How tough it had really become, and there's no doubt about it.

This was not justice as far as Cochran was concerned. "When they load up, when they rush to judgment, we have to keep pointing that out. It's not un-American to do that. I'm not afraid to do it."

Cochran saw in Combs a kind, generous, and extremely talented young man who could be faulted for bad judgment, but who should not have faced the possibility of 15 years in prison. The attorney went back on his promise never to defend another criminal case.

A NIGHT ON THE TOWN GOES TERRIBLY WRONG

The events leading to Combs' arrest began on December 27, 1999. Combs was at his house in the Hamptons, an exclusive beach area at the tip of Long Island in New York. The plan for the next day was a vacation with then-girlfriend Jennifer Lopez in the Caribbean, but there was still a full night for partying ahead. They left the Hamptons and headed to Midtown Manhattan with rapper Jamaal "Shyne" Barrow, whom Combs was guiding toward a contract with his record label. Bodyguard Anthony "Wolf" Jones and driver Wardell Fenderson accompanied them.

They sought out a good time in the VIP section of Club New York, enjoying themselves in style. While squeezing through the crowd to leave, Shyne Barrow accidentally jostled against Matthew "Scar" Allen.

On prison terms, even a mere bump calls for some form of retaliation. Perhaps Allen, an ex-con, was still living by prison rules. Or, perhaps Allen and others watching the Combs entourage were jealous. In any event, an argument escalated into gunplay between Barrow, Allen, and a few others in the crowded nightspot. Luckily no one was killed, but several people sustained injuries. It was impossible to tell whose weapon caused those wounds.

Some witnesses said that Combs contributed to the gunfire, which he emphatically denied. He told everyone who would listen that he did not own a gun. He had seen too many loved ones die from gunshots, his father included, to even consider owning a gun. That did not stop prosecutors from holding Combs accountable for weapons they said had been in his Lincoln Navigator.

A gun was supposedly found under the front passenger seat, which had been occupied by the bodyguard. Another gun

Hip-hop star Jamaal "Shyne" Barrow, pictured above, was arrested following a shooting in a New York nightclub. Shyne had jostled against ex-con Matthew "Scar" Allen, prompting a gunfight that resulted in injuries but no deaths.

was recovered and turned in to the police days later by a man who said it was thrown from a passing SUV. A third weapon, the only one recovered that had been discharged, was reportedly found on Shyne when the police arrested him inside the club.

Witnesses from that night testified to Puffy's participation in the shooting, but this was not as simple as it sounded. Those testifying against the rapper were involved in lawsuits worth $1 billion collectively, which might have made them biased.

The one witness without a lawsuit initially alleged that Combs was involved in the shooting, but she became less adamant by the end of Ben Brafman's cross-examination. This witness, initially thought credible, had based her conclusion on news reports and conversations with other people as much as on what she had actually seen in the chaos.

Cochran brought the savvy, hard-nosed Brafman into the case because Brafman knew New York criminal law and the local bigshots in the field. Investigator Hinkson worked closely with the new team in preparing the defense.

Their work paid off when they coaxed a security guard at the club into court. This security guard worked at the Department of Social Services by day and did not want to testify. She hated to get involved in the media circus, but her concern over an innocent man being convicted won out. On the stand, she confidently reiterated that Combs did not have a gun in the club and did not fire one. She knew this because she fell on top of him when the shooting started and covered him until it was safe enough to show him to the exit. Lopez and Combs had made a hasty retreat from the scene. They sped up Eighth Avenue with their bodyguard and driver. The police gave pursuit until the Lincoln Navigator was stopped about a half-mile away from the club.

WILL JUSTICE BE DONE?

No matter how confident the defense is about a case, it is impossible to know what a jury will decide. Cochran said that, behind the scenes, his client was a scared kid. Combs feared being separated from his family and his life. He controlled those fears while on the stand and made a strong declaration of innocence. At the same time, he remained protective of the men who partied with him at Club New York. Despite his fear of conviction, Combs refused to let his attorneys do anything that would jeopardize Shyne's claim of self-defense.

The aspiring recording artist had not been looking for trouble; just the opposite. Shyne had been recently assaulted

IN HIS OWN WORDS...

Cochran believed he served justice when innocent people go free and guilty people are accountable for their indiscretions. He saw no need to ask his clients about their innocence or guilt. In his work, the innocent were quick to express their innocence and the guilty talked about the best possible plea bargain. Cochran summarized his thoughts on true justice in *A Lawyer's Life*:

> There is one thing that remains as true today as it was when this country was founded: If one man cannot get a fair trial, no matter how hideous his crime or evil the man, none of us can be certain of getting a fair trial.

by a group of people in Brooklyn and began carrying the gun for protection. He would pay the price for his actions with a conviction and a 10-year jail sentence. While serving his time, Shyne signed a multimillion-dollar record contract with Island Def Jam Records.

Chauffeur Wardell Fenderson came through the incident practically unscathed. He cut a deal with the district attorney, claiming Combs bribed him to say the gun in the car belonged to either him or Jones. The $3 million lawsuit he filed against his employer impacted his credibility, as did the fact that before the alleged bribe, he did state that the gun belonged to bodyguard Wolf Jones.

Sean Combs, Shyne Barrow, and Jones were tried together, but retained separate attorneys paid by Combs. He spent about $1 million for their defense. At its end in 2001, he sat next to his lawyers holding a Bible and had photos of his children spread in front of him as the jury entered with the verdicts. He waited, unsure if he would go home to his family. The jury cleared Sean Combs and his bodyguard of all charges.

Cochran left the courtroom smiling about his client's success. He declared that the "five not-guilty verdicts will resound in my ears forever." Although he did not tell reporters, the stress of those criminal proceedings were enough to last a lifetime.

Sean Combs experienced an epiphany of sorts. "I've changed, I've matured," he told *Time* magazine. "This whole thing has made me deeper." He spent time with his children and

Cochran is shown here with Sean "Puffy" Combs. With Cochran's help, Combs and his bodyguard were cleared of all charges after a shooting in a New York nightclub.

evaluated his future. From this deeper reflection, Sean "P. Diddy" Combs emerged. Cochran hoped his friend had learned to protect this new image and to choose his associates wisely.

Unlike Combs, Cochran's double-duty on the Dorismond lawsuit and other cases did not allow him time for personal reflection. He already understood what his life was about. He believed, "I'm not free until everybody is free or have an opportunity to be the best they can be."

10

"And Yet I Swear This Oath—America Will Be!"

Johnnie L. Cochran, Jr., an imperfect man, sought continual improvement for himself and his community, just as his parents taught him. Through his parent's boundless optimism he envisioned goodness rising from the imperfections in and around him. No matter how great or small the flaws may have been, he believed that all it took was hard work and a plan to polish them into something deserving of pride.

Hard work and a plan carried him to what he believed was the apex of his career. Before the Simpson trial, he was almost done with the law; afterward, his thoughts of putting the law aside and gradually retiring from hard work to peace and comfort resurfaced. Instead he continued on his compelling quest for a better society, from Los Angeles County and Washington, D.C., to all 50 states. This pace came as no surprise to Dale Mason Cochran. She never believed her husband would retire. Pursuing his mission bolstered every fiber of his being.

His was an impressive feat. The money and the comfort it brought, on a personal level, were pure joy. On a business level, damages paid to his clients sent a message that any leader in government and private industry could understand: Do better by the people, or Cochran would deprive them of their funds and place the money in more compassionate hands.

JUSTICE EVERYWHERE

With the Cochran Firm, he could spread this message nation-wide. It did not matter if problems rested in corporate America or some other institution. He wanted to see justice done. The arrogance of some police offenders simply made them an easy target.

"People in New York and Los Angeles," he stated, "especially mothers in the African-American community, are more afraid of the police injuring or killing their children than they are of muggers on the corner."

Tyisha Miller of Riverside, California, was such a person. She was killed by police officers that her cousin had called for help. The cousin had come to assist Tyisha with a flat tire and found her unconscious, locked in her car. A policeman broke through the teen's car windshield, startling her awake. When she allegedly reached for her gun for protection, her life was

IN HIS OWN WORDS...

Los Angeles Times staff writer BettiJane Levine noted portions of a speech made by Cochran in 2002:

Let me tell you the bottom line. Whether Chicago, Atlanta or D.C.—or wherever I have offices—I want to change the culture. I want to reverse things so the bad cops fear the good cops. The way it is now, the bad cops have the run of the place. There is this blue wall of silence. Nobody will tell on anybody. Nobody will testify.

Demonstrators including Dr. Martin Luther King III (second from left) and the Reverend Al Sharpton (third from left) march in Riverside, California, after the district attorney's office said the four police officers involved in the shooting death of Tyisha Miller would not be held criminally responsible.

taken. Although the officers were never prosecuted, *People* reported that the police chief there believed "their actions were not reasonable." Poor judgment may have been the triggering factor, but this was the measure of Johnnie Cochran's career: forcing people with poor judgment to re-examine their actions and take a better course in the future.

Cochran's vision was not to set the world ablaze or even make it colorblind. He hoped to craft a system that respected people for their differences and protected their right to be different under the U.S. Constitution. He believed everyone deserved a system that made choices to preserve life, not take it. Failing that, individuals abusing the law deserved to have their authority revoked. If reducing their bank accounts was the way to get his message across, Cochran was not afraid to do it. In the latter years of his life, Cochran carried a caseload of 50 lawsuits on any given day. A private jet lifted him to where he needed to be. Peter Neufeld told *New York* magazine, "He's got the speed gene."

He seemed to have his hand in every major lawsuit in the nation. Some detractors called him a case-stealer. Other critics believed he only cared for one race, and still more said his growing law firm was really about growing money. None of the characterizations were entirely accurate, for he had the strength of his convictions.

COLLABORATIVE EFFORTS

The Cochran Firm was built on individual mergers and partnerships with firms willing to serve clients without respect to wealth, race, or gender. The firm concentrated on civil cases where the most social justice could be accomplished. Where needed, Cochran collaborated on strategies and other lawyers worked the details. Few attorneys had mastered his level of cooperation with such a wide corps of attorneys.

Cochran never solicited clients. They chose his services, sometimes over the objections of existing attorneys and sometimes not. Either way, if a case had social merit, he was willing to take it. The issue of eminent domain and government seizure of private property was one troubling concept to him and this issue was not limited to race.

He contested the notion of eminent domain, such as when the Ernest N. Morial Convention Center in New Orleans acquired Tchoupitoulas Warehouse over the objection of its owner and resident Dr. Steve Lesser. Cochran worked to achieve a $10.5 million verdict in his client's favor in 2003.

Cochran saw a conflict in the government's ability to seize property of a person facing drug charges. An attempted government seizure in California ended in the death of million-aire Donald Scott in 1992. His widow, Frances Plante, refused to leave the Ventura ranch despite her house burning down. She moved into a tepee and waited for Cochran and Eric Ferrer, from his Los Angeles office, to resolve the protracted battle. In between work on the Louima and Diallo cases in New York, the two attorneys reached a $5 million settlement with the government agencies involved.

SUCCESSES CONTINUE

Cochran established a long list of successes in negotiations, first with the Los Angeles police force—the ban on the choke-hold and eventual restructuring of the LAPD and Signal Hill, for instance. Then came others.

The New Jersey state troopers were notorious among the black community for racial profiling. African Americans typically warned one another before driving the South Jersey section of the New Jersey Turnpike. In 1998, four young minority men were stopped on the turnpike without cause and then were fired upon by state troopers. Before the incident, the four aspired to win basketball scholarships to North Carolina Central University. After the shooting, they hoped to pull their lives back together. Cochran negotiated $2.95 million to help them do that. The state overhauled police procedures and restructured the state police from the top down. Criminal charges against 128 people, stemming from questionable traffic stops, were dropped as a result of questionable procedures discovered during Cochran's investigation.

Cochran later represented 13 black New Jersey state troopers in a racial harassment suit against their employer. The state settled the case, giving $4 million to the troopers and $1 million toward attorneys' fees.

A settlement was reached with Michigan firefighters in 2002 that compensated African Americans and women for past discrimination in work assignments and paved the way for equal duties in the future. Cochran used the law to deliver the equity that was rightfully theirs.

In Montgomery County, Maryland, the police have cameras in their cars and other equipment because one of Cochran's clients set aside half of a $2 million settlement for such improvements. "It's a tool," he said, "to be used to ensure that the promises of our democracy are available to all of us equally. At least, at its most eloquent that is what it is supposed to be."

LEGAL RAINBOW

Partners and employees of the Cochran Firm span all races and both genders. They represent Cochran's vision of the level playing field he wished to see throughout America. The color of a client's skin, likewise, never was as important to him as the nature of the case. It showed when he accepted the cause of Reginald Denny, a white truck driver caught in the wave of violence during the 1992 Los Angeles riots. Many African Americans in Los Angeles did not want Cochran to pit himself against the local minority for the benefit of a white man.

The beatings of Denny and several other drivers were taped by a TV news team roving in a helicopter above the riots. The 911 emergency dispatch was flooded with thousands of calls for help from TV viewers, but the police did not come to the victims' rescue. Good Samaritans in the neighborhood dashed out of their homes and saved the victims from possible death.

Cochran was not sure what could be done to help Denny and make the police more responsive to citizens in Watts. He needed a legal basis for Denny's personal injury suit and those of a Latino and a Japanese American beaten at the same location, as well as a suit for the first young man killed that day. The police's failure to respond to the flood of 911 calls

Cochran appeared on *The Phil Donohue Show* in 1993 with his client Reginald Denny (second from left), who was beaten during the 1992 Los Angeles riots. After watching a videotape of the attack, assailant Henry Keith Watson (far right) apologized for the assault and was forgiven by Denny.

became his link. Their case was dismissed twice. He settled for helping Denny receive workman's compensation benefits, and Bill Cosby volunteered to pay for daughter Ashley Denny's education.

In 2003, Cochran topped the award in the famed Erin Brockovich pollution case against Pacific Gas and Electric almost twofold. An award of $700 million was given to 18,000 people in their personal injury case against a chemical-production corporation over a toxic chemical dumping site. Of the award, $50 million was put aside for site cleanup in Anniston, Alabama.

His firm also assumed less publicized cases, such as one in 2003 involving seven people who died in an office building fire in Chicago. Civil charges were levied against the building contractor and his partner. Faulty electrical wiring on the twelfth floor was suspected of starting the fire.

Cochran continued his celebrity representation as well. Among others, two similar cases surfaced for alleged name infringement: Spike Lee sued Viacom for the proposed Spike TV channel in 2003, and Rosa Parks sued rap artists OutKast and their label, LaFace Records. He also represented NBA basketball star Latrell Sprewell, formerly of the Golden State Warriors, after the athlete's fight with his coach.

GIVING BACK

Cochran loved his legal successes and the money they brought. He never denied enjoying the trappings of wealth—luxury cars, homes, colorful clothes with monogrammed cuffs, and a corporate jet at his disposal. He reveled in highbrow social gatherings that accrued with his celebrity image, and showed his New York office how to have a 2,000-guest party. Cochran literally belonged to the prestigious Inner Circle—that is the Inner Circle of Advocates (the 100 top plaintiff lawyers in the United States).

In the midst of this good life, he never forgot that the financial status he so enjoyed ultimately came from average Americans. He gave back by opening a toll-free line to his offices around the country.

Cochran and his wife contributed $250,000 of his earnings to build 10 townhouses for homeless families in Los Angeles. Syd Irmas donated the land and the Johnnie L. Cochran, Sr., and Hattie B. Cochran Villa opened in 1991. Cochran and wife Dale Mason served on the board of the Los Angeles Family Housing Corp. and could not think of a better way to spend their money.

In Buffalo, New York, donations from Cochran and attorney Bob Perk established a day-care center to honor their client Cynthia Wiggins, who had been a struggling single mother.

He and his wife created the Johnnie L. Cochran Art Foundation and seeded its endowment with $250,000. "I'm big on art as a bridge between communities," he told Nina Burleigh. "So I not only do the legal stuff. I try to do things in the community. Church-art-community: that's my thing." He and wife Dale generously gave time and money to all three.

During the height of his popularity, he tried to accommodate as many of the 15 to 20 daily requests for personal appearances as possible. When he did, crowds swarmed around to congratulate his dedication and seek his services. He remained gracious to them all.

His love for community led him to a number of board memberships. Chairing the Upper Manhattan Empowerment

IN HIS OWN WORDS...

Johnnie L. Cochran, Jr. expressed his feelings about the worth of his profession in his autobiography *A Lawyer's Life*:

I set out as a young lawyer to change the world. The fact is that lawyers...are doing exactly that. Lawyers are making multibillion-dollar corporations responsible for their actions. Lawyers are saving lives by forcing companies to clean up the poisonous mess they've made of our environment. They are forcing companies to admit the products they market can be deadly. They are forcing manufacturers to add safety devices and do the extra testing necessary to ensure that their products can be used safely....

I've gotten myself involved in cases that have the potential to change thousands of lives.... There are still many days when the injustice I see makes me angry. Days when the racial injustice and politically conservative nature of the system frustrates me. And fortunately, days when the system works just exactly the way it was designed, and provides justice for the people....

I loved it the first day I went to work as a lawyer. I love it still. And I know without any doubt that I will love it always. I have heard all the jokes, I laughed at many of them myself and I am so proud to have spent my life as a lawyer.

I rest my case.

Cochran signs copies of his book *Journey to Justice* at an appearance at Stanford University in California. The book was his first autobiography.

Zone ushered in a new Harlem renaissance in New York. Perhaps the role he played on the coordinating committee for reparations for descendants of African-American slaves had the greatest potential to effect generations of people into the future, not from miniscule payments to masses of African Americans but through endowments, educational and otherwise.

A LIFE FULFILLED

In 2003, Cochran's health began to fail. That December, he was diagnosed with a brain tumor. In April 2004, he underwent surgery in an attempt to remove some or all of the tumor. At the time, he described his ailment as a neurological condition that required a procedure. After the surgery, the limelight-loving lawyer began to avoid the media, until September, when he told the *New York Post* that he would be getting back into the swing of work with a major expansion of the Cochran Firm.

It was not to be. On Tuesday, March 29, 2005, Cochran died at home from complications arising from the brain tumor. His family was nearby. Before that, though, he did have time to settle his personal affairs.

Patty Sikora's lawsuit against him for allegedly breaking a 1983 property agreement was resolved in 2004. More important, his daughter Tiffany was married to Javarro Michael Edwards in a lovely ceremony at her alma mater, Pepperdine University, in Malibu. After being escorted down the aisle on her father's arm, she took Edwards's hands and exchanged vows in front of 230 happy guests.

It is hard to imagine what more could have been accomplished in Johnnie Cochran's lifetime. He partied with the best of them and expressed his love for people in several languages. He made cameo appearances in several movies and produced others. As far as his legal career is concerned, he achieved what, on paper, looked to be impossible.

Johnnie Cochran died believing in the declaration of Martin Luther King, Jr., that "an injustice anywhere is a threat to justice everywhere." Like the Reverend King, he knew the world could do better. He is gone, but his legacy lives in the Cochran Firm, in the lives saved, in the art funded and, of course, in his family. Perhaps the achievement for which he will be remembered most is carrying the social justice movement to new heights—he was the people's advocate.

1937 Born October 2 in Shreveport, Louisiana, to Hattie Bass Cochran and Johnnie L. Cochran, Sr.

1942 The Cochran family leaves Shreveport for the San Francisco area

1948 Cochrans relocate to San Diego, then settle in Los Angeles a year later

1950 Johnnie attends prestigious Los Angeles High School

1954 Thurgood Marshall wins *Brown v. Board of Education*

1959 Cochran graduates from the University of California, Los Angeles, with a bachelor's degree in business administration.

1960 Marries Barbara Berry

1962 Daughter Melodie is born

1963 Passes California Bar; becomes a deputy city attorney

1965 Opens the Law Office of Johnnie L. Cochran, Jr.

1966 Firm becomes Cochran, Atkins & Evans.

1969 Second daughter Tiffany is born

1970 Loses Leonard Deadwyler civil case

1972 Loses murder case representing Black Panther Elmer "Geronimo" Pratt; vows never to stop working to free his friend

1973 Has son Jonathan with Patty Sikora

1977 Is named Criminal Trial Lawyer of the Year by Los Angeles Criminal Courts Bar Association

1978 Joins the district attorney's office; divorces Barbara Berry

1979 Helps found Los Angeles County's Domestic Violence Council

1980 Leaves district attorney's office

1981 Wins an unprecedented $760,000 and government reform from a California municipality for the death of Ron Settles while in police custody

1982 The Mincey case succeeds in getting police choke hold outlawed

1985 Marries Dale Mason

1990 Is named Civil Trial Lawyer of the Year by Los Angeles Trial Lawyers Association

1991 Represents Reginald Oliver Denny, a white truck driver severely beaten by angry mob in Watts during Los Angeles riots; Washington office expanded to Cochran, Mitchell & Loftkin

1992 Wins highest jury award from Los Angeles to that date, $9.4 million for a 13-year-old Latino girl molested by an LAPD police officer

1993 Negotiates a settlement for Michael Jackson against the claim of child molestation

1995 Trial of Century—acquittal in the O.J. Simpson murder trial transforms Cochran into national figure

1996 *Journey to Justice,* his autobiography, is published

1997 Pratt murder and assault conviction are overturned; Court TV show launched; negotiates $8.75 million settlement for Abner Louima and reforms in police practice

2001 Successfully defends Sean Combs against weapons and bribery charges, Cochran's last criminal case

2002 His autobiography *A Lawyer's Life,* is published; represents former Enron employees, and Spike Lee and Rosa Parks in separate name-infringement cases

2004 Settles palimony suit brought against him by Sikora; Tiffany Cochran marries; is treated for an inoperable brain tumor

2005 Dies of a brain tumor March 29 at 12:30 P.M. in his Los Angeles home

BOOKS

Bauerlein, Mark, Ph.D., Todd Steven Burroughs Ph. D., Ella Forbes, Ph.D., et al. *Civil Rights Chronicle: The African-American Struggle for Freedom.* Lincolnwood, Ill.: Legacy Publishing, a division of Publication International, Ltd., 2003.

Berry, Barbara Cochran and Joanne Parrent. *Life After Johnnie Cochran: Why I Left the Sweetest-Talking, Most Successful Black Lawyer in L.A.* New York: Basic Books, 1995.

Blaustein, Albert P. and Robert L. Zangrando, *Civil Rights and the American Negro: A Documentary History.* New York: Washington Square Press, 1968.

Bronstad, Amanda. "Ex-Cochran client wants to complain." *Los Angeles Business Journal,* April 5, 2004.

Cochran, Johnnie and David Fisher. *A Lawyer's Life.* New York: Thomas Dunne Books, St. Martin's Press, 2002.

Cochran, Johnnie L. and Tim Rutten. *Journey to Justice.* New York: One World, Ballantine Books, 1996.

"Defense superstar Johnnie Cochran dead at 67." The Associated Press, March 30, 2005.

"Johnnie Cochran files suit in Oklahoma City on behalf of four survivors." *Jet,* May 29, 1995.

"Johnnie Cochran settles record-setting $700 mil. pollution case." *Jet,* Sept. 15, 2003.

Keyes, Allison J., Gloria Blakely, et al. *Great African Americans.* Lincolnwood, Ill.: Publications International, Ltd., 2002

Lambert, Pam. "Defending Dad." *People Weekly* April 10, 1995.

Montagne, Renee. "Analysis: Disgruntled ex-client's suit against Johnnie Cochran goes to U.S. Supreme Court." *Morning Edition* (NPR), March 22, 2005.

"P. Diddy, Warner Music Ink Joint Venture." *The Associated Press,* April 16, 2005

"Puffy a changed man after trial." The Associated Press, March 19, 2001.

Randolph, Laura B. "Best in the West." *Ebony*, April 1994.

"S.C. Allows 'Palimony' Action Against Johnnie Cochran to Proceed." *Metropolitan News Enterprise*, August 30, 2001

Simon, Scott. "Interview Gil Garcetti." *Weekend Edition Saturday* (NPR), June 21, 2004.

U.S. Riot Commission Report. Report of the National Advisory Commission on Civil Disorders. New York: Bantam Book Edition, 1968.

WEBSITES

African American Literature Book Club—Johnnie Cochran
www.aalbc.com/authors/johnnie_cochran.htm

Black Entertainment and Sports Lawyers Association—Johnnie Cochran
www.besla.org/johnnie_tribute.aspx

The Cochran Firm
www.cochranfirm.com

Court TV Online
www.courttv.com/trials

PBS Frontline—L.A.P.D. blues: the scandal
www.pbs.org/wgbh/pages/frontline/shows/lapd/scandal/audio.html

page:

2: Associated Press, AP	71: Associated Press, AP
8: Associated Press, AP	78: Associated Press, AP
12: Lake County Museum/CORBIS	89: Associated Press, AP
17: Associated Press, AP	93: Associated Press, AP
27: Associated Press, AP	102: Associated Press, AP
33: Reprinted by permission of Loyola School of Law	107: Associated Press, AP
	112: Associated Press, AP
37: Bettmann/CORBIS	115: Getty Images
41: Associated Press, AP	119: Associated Press, AP
46: Associated Press, AP	123: Associated Press, AP
61: Associated Press, AP	126: Associated Press, AP

cover: Time Life Pictures/Getty Images

Gloria Blakely is a journalist and history lover. She has written or contributed to several books for Chelsea House, including *Condoleezza Rice, Danny Glover, Muhammad Ali, Jesse Jackson,* and *Rosa Parks.* Blakely graduated from the Howard University honors program and is a member of the Philadelphia Association of Black Journalists in Philadelphia, where she resides. Other literary credits include the Publications International, Ltd., anthology *Great African Americans,* which she co-authored, as well as numerous publications in newspapers and national magazines, including *Essence, Upscale,* and *Pathfinders Travel.* She is listed among up-and-coming children's book writers in *Something About the Authors* by Gale Services, and she received two writing awards at the 2003 Philadelphia Writers' Conference.